The Nature of Morality

The nature of morality

AN INTRODUCTION TO ETHICS

GILBERT HARMAN

Princeton University

New York
OXFORD UNIVERSITY PRESS
1977

For Elizabeth

Preface

This book is a philosophical introduction to ethics. It differs from existing texts by focusing on a basic philosophical problem about morality, its apparent immunity from observational testing. Other texts either ignore this issue altogether, in order to concentrate on interesting but largely nonphilosophical discussions of moral problems, or treat the issue as only one of several highly technical questions in something called "meta-ethics."

Meta-ethics became a subject during the period of linguistic philosophy, say from 1930 to 1960, when many English-speaking philosophers toyed with the idea that philosophy might be nothing but the analysis of language. Philosophical ethics, in this view, was the analysis of the language of morals. The philosophical subject of meta-ethics was to be distinguished from the nonphilosophical subject of normative ethics. A normative ethical theory would be a theory of Right and Wrong, Good and Evil, Ought and Ought Not. It would be a nonlinguistic and therefore nonphilosophical subject. A meta-ethical theory, on the other hand, would be a properly philosophical account of the meaning and justification of moral judgments such as those that might be made in the course of setting out a normative ethical theory.

Many philosophers now think that this sort of distinction rests on highly controversial and possibly even incoherent assumptions about meaning and justification. But at the time these assumptions were treated as self-evident principles that had to be mastered by any student of the subject and the basic philosophical problems of ethics were replaced by a series of questions about meaning. As the main issues were forgotten, ethics became uninteresting and by 1960 work in meta-ethics had just about come to an end.

Meanwhile, the assumptions of linguistic philosophy had been under attack. Philosophers began to believe again that philosophy need not be restricted to the analysis of language. This meant that philosophical ethics did not have to restrict itself to meta-ethics. Indeed, arguments by W. V. Quine and other philosophers actually undermined the supposed distinction between meta-ethics and normative ethics by showing that there can be no real separation between questions of substance and questions of meaning.

This last point was not immediately appreciated, however. What was immediately clear was that philosophical ethics did not have to be identified with meta-ethics. It was less clear, at first, that the whole distinction between meta-ethics and normative ethics had to be abandoned. Philosophers might at this stage have tried to take on the basic problem about morality without the meta-ethical baggage that had previously hindered such an attempt. Not seeing how to do that, however, they retained the distinction between normative and meta-ethics and turned to various questions of normative ethics, discussing at first the claims of utilitarianism (see Chapter 13), then various nonutilitarian principles, more recently, the details of particular moral issues, such as war, abortion, and equality. This has often been interesting but has less often had much to do with philosophy. And philosophers have had little to say in recent years about the basic problem about morality, the seeming irrelevance of observational evidence.

One result has been that introductory courses in ethics, and the textbooks and anthologies designed for such courses, have become more interesting but less philosophical. Students spend less time thinking about technical questions of meta-ethics and more time grappling with the moral issues of the day. Courses in ethics are more "relevant" and students are more "involved." It may even be true that these courses are doing some good; perhaps students learn something; perhaps their powers of analysis are improved. (Probably not!) But students in such courses are not really studying philosophy. The basic philosophical issues are not being addressed. Consequently, these courses and books are unsatisfying even though interesting and "relevant."

Why has this happened? In part it has happened because meta-ethics had become so uninteresting and because philosophers of ethics have been slow to appreciate the true significance of the arguments that undermined the old linguistic philosophy. Another factor has been the increased concern of teachers and students with social issues. They have wanted to spend more of their time discussing such issues and have been delighted to think that they could legitimately do so in the classroom. The unhappy effect has been a decline in the philosophical content of courses in ethics and the books designed for use in such courses.

I hope this book will help reverse this decline. I have focused on a basic *philosophical* issue. Where various other questions arise, I have indicated how they are related to this basic issue. I have avoided purely technical questions that have no direct bearing on the main issue; it is too easy to be sidetracked. In particular, I simply avoid the meta-ethical apparatus of an earlier time.

Some textbooks pretend to set out a number of philosophical positions in a neutral way, letting the reader decide between them. This gives, I think, a misleading impression of philosophy. Philosophy aims at understanding. In ethics, for example, you must try to develop an overall account of the nature of morality. That is what I have attempted in this book. Although I discuss a variety of views, it will be clear what my own position is. The book as a whole represents a sustained defense of that position. I assume that the reader will not be convinced; but I hope that he or she will be led to try to develop a more adequate account.

I am indebted to Judy Jarvis Thomson for many comments and suggestions about Chapters 1 through 10; and Jim Anderson of Oxford University Press gave me much useful advice, for which I am grateful. I am indebted in a different way to a fellowship from the American Council of Learned Societies, which gave me the time to write this book.

I have occasionally borrowed arguments and examples from "Moral Relativism Defended," *Philosophical Review*, Volume 84 (1975), pages 3–22. Chapter 10 previously appeared in *Crítica* Volume VII, Number 21 (1975). Chapter 11 was published in Dianoia Number XXI (1975) in a Spanish translation by Hugo Margain,"Una teoria naturalista de las razones."

Princeton, New Jersey   G. H.
September 1976

Contents

I

The problem with ethics

1 Ethics and observation

1. The basic issue

Can moral principles be tested and confirmed in the way scientific principles can? Consider the principle that, if you are given a choice between five people alive and one dead or five people dead and one alive, you should always choose to have five people alive and one dead rather than the other way round. We can easily imagine examples that appear to confirm this principle. Here is one:

You are a doctor in a hospital's emergency room when six accident victims are brought in. All six are in danger of dying but one is much worse off than the others. You can just barely save that person if you devote all of your resources to him and let the others die. Alternatively, you can save the other five if you are willing to ignore the most seriously injured person.

It would seem that in this case you, the doctor, would be right to save the five and let the other person die. So this example, taken by itself, confirms the principle under consideration. Next, consider the following case.

You have five patients in the hospital who are dying, each in need of a separate organ. One needs a kidney, another a lung, a third a heart, and so forth. You can save all five if you take a single healthy person and remove his heart, lungs, kidneys, and so forth, to distribute to these five patients. Just such a healthy person is in room 306. He is in the hospital for routine tests. Having seen his test results, you know that he is perfectly healthy and of the right tissue compatibility. If you do nothing, he will survive without incident; the other patients will die, however. The other five patients can be saved only if the person in Room 306 is cut up and his organs distributed. In that case, there would be one dead but five saved.

The principle in question tells us that you should cut up the patient in Room 306. But in this case, surely you must not sacrifice this innocent bystander, even to save the five other patients. Here a moral principle has been tested and disconfirmed in what may seem to be a surprising way.

This, of course, was a "thought experiment." We did not really compare a hypothesis with the world. We compared an explicit principle with our feelings about certain imagined examples. In the same way, a physicist performs thought experiments in order to compare explicit hypotheses with his "sense" of what should happen in certain situations, a "sense" that he has acquired as a result of his long working familiarity with current theory. But scientific hypotheses can also be tested in real experiments, out in the world.

Can moral principles be tested in the same way, out in the world? You can observe someone do something, but can you ever perceive the rightness or wrongness of what he does? If you round a corner and see a group of young hoodlums pour gasoline on a cat and ignite it, you do not need to *conclude* that what they are doing is wrong; you do not need to figure anything out; you can *see* that it is wrong. But is your reaction due to the actual wrongness of what you see or is it simply a reflection of your moral "sense," a "sense" that you have acquired perhaps as a result of your moral upbringing?

2. Observation

The issue is complicated. There are no pure observations. Observations are always "theory laden." What you perceive depends to some extent on the theory you hold, consciously or unconsciously. You see some children pour gasoline on a cat and ignite it. To really see that, you have to possess a great deal of knowledge, know about a considerable number of objects, know about people: that people pass through the life stages infant, baby, child, adolescent, adult. You must know what flesh and blood animals are, and in particular, cats. You must have some idea of life. You must know what gasoline is, what burning is, and much more. In one sense, what you "see" is a pattern of light on your retina, a shifting array of splotches, although even that is theory, and you could never adequately describe what you see in that sense. In another sense, you see what you do because of the theories you hold. Change those theories and you would see something else, given the same pattern of light.

Similarly, if you hold a moral view, whether it is held consciously or unconsciously, you will be able to perceive rightness or wrongness, goodness or badness, justice or injustice. There is no difference in this respect between moral propositions and other theoretical propositions. If there is a difference, it must be found elsewhere.

Observation depends on theory because perception involves forming a belief as a fairly direct result of observing something; you can form a belief only if you understand the relevant concepts and a concept is what it is by virtue of its role in some theory or system of beliefs. To recognize a child as a child is to employ, consciously or unconsciously, a concept that is defined by its place in a framework of the stages of human life. Similarly, burning is an empty concept apart from its theoretical connections to the concepts of heat, destruction, smoke, and fire.

Moral concepts—Right and Wrong, Good and Bad, Justice and Injustice—also have a place in your theory or system of beliefs and are the concepts they are because of their context. If we say that observation has occurred whenever an opinion is a direct result of perception, we must allow that there is moral observation, because such an opinion can be a moral opinion as easily as any other sort. In this sense, observation may be used to confirm or disconfirm moral theories. The observational opinions that, in this sense, you find yourself with can be in either agreement or conflict with your consciously explicit moral principles. When they are in conflict, you must choose between your explicit theory and observation. In ethics, as in science, you sometimes opt for theory, and say that you made an error in observation or were biased or whatever, or you sometimes opt for observation, and modify your theory.

In other words, in both science and ethics, general principles are invoked to explain particular cases and, therefore, in both science and ethics, the general principles you accept can be tested by appealing to particular judgments that certain things are right or wrong, just or unjust, and so forth; and these judgments are analogous to direct perceptual judgments about facts.

3. Observational evidence

Nevertheless, observation plays a role in science that it does not seem to play in ethics. The difference is that you need to make assumptions about certain physical facts to explain the occurrence of the observations that support a scientific theory, but you do not seem to need to make assumptions about any moral facts to explain the occurrence of the so-called moral observations I have been talking about. In the moral case, it would seem that you need only make assumptions about the psychology or moral sensibility of the person making the moral observation. In the scientific case, theory is tested against the world.

The point is subtle but important. Consider a physicist making an observation to test a scientific theory. Seeing a vapor trail in a cloud chamber, he thinks, "There goes a proton." Let us suppose that this is an observation in the relevant sense, namely, an immediate judgment made in response to the situation without any conscious reasoning having taken place. Let us also suppose that his observation confirms his theory, a theory that helps give meaning to the very term "proton" as it occurs in his observational judgment. Such a confirmation rests on inferring an explanation. He can count his making the observation as confirming evidence for his theory only to the extent that it is reasonable to explain his making the observation by assuming that, not only is he in a certain psychological "set," given the theory he accepts and his beliefs about the experimental apparatus, but furthermore, there really was a proton going through the cloud chamber, causing the vapor trail, which he saw as a proton. (This is evidence for the theory to the extent that the theory can explain the proton's being there better than competing theories can.) But, if his having made that observation could have been equally well explained by his psychological set alone, without the need for any assumption about a proton, then the observation would not have been evidence for the existence of that proton and therefore would not have been evidence for the theory. His making the observation supports the theory only because, in order to explain his making the observation, it is reasonable to assume something about the world over and above the assumptions made about the observer's psychology. In particular, it is reasonable to assume that there was a proton going through the cloud chamber, causing the vapor trail.

Compare this case with one in which you make a moral judgment immediately and without conscious reasoning, say, that the children are wrong to set the cat on fire or that the doctor would be wrong to cut up one healthy patient to save five dying patients. In order to explain your making the first of these judgments, it would be reasonable to assume, perhaps, that the children really are pouring gasoline on a cat and you are seeing them do it. But, in neither case is there any obvious reason to assume anything about "moral facts," such as that it really is wrong to set the cat on fire or to cut up the patient in Room 306. Indeed, an assumption about moral facts would seem to be totally irrelevant to the explanation of your making the judgment you make. It would seem that all we need assume is that you have certain more or less well articulated moral principles that are reflected in the judgments you make, based on your moral sensibility. It seems to be completely irrelevant to our explanation whether your intuitive immediate judgment is true or false.

The observation of an event can provide observational evidence for or against a scientific theory in the sense that the truth of that observation can be relevant to a reasonable explanation of why that observation was made. A moral observation does not seem, in the same sense, to be observational evidence for or against any moral theory, since the truth or falsity of the moral observation seems to be completely irrelevant to any reasonable explanation of why that observation was made. The fact that an observation of an event was made at the time it was made is evidence not only about the observer but also about the physical facts. The fact that you made a particular moral observation when you did does not seem to be evidence about moral facts, only evidence about you and your moral sensibility. Facts about protons can affect what you observe, since a proton passing through the cloud chamber can cause a vapor trail that reflects light to your eye in a way that, given your scientific training and psychological set, leads you to judge that what you see is a proton. But there does not seem to be any way in which the actual rightness or wrongness of a given situation can have any effect on your perceptual apparatus. In this respect, ethics seems to differ from science.

In considering whether moral principles can help explain observations, it is therefore important to note an ambiguity in the word "observation." You see the children set the cat on fire and immediately think, "That's wrong." In one sense, your observation is that what the children are doing is wrong. In another sense, your observation is your thinking that thought. Moral observations might explain observations in the first sense but not in the second sense. Certain moral principles might help to explain why it was *wrong* of the children to set the cat on fire, but moral principles seem to be of no help in explaining *your thinking* that that is wrong. In the first sense of "observation," moral principles can be tested by observation—"That this act is wrong is evidence that causing unnecessary suffering is wrong." But in the second sense of "observation," moral principles cannot clearly be tested by observation, since they do not appear to help explain observations in this second sense of "observation." Moral principles do not seem to help explain your observing what you observe.

Of course, if you are already given the moral principle that it is wrong to cause unnecessary suffering, you can take your seeing the children setting the cat on fire as observational evidence that they are doing something wrong. Similarly, you can suppose that your seeing the vapor trail is observational evidence that a proton is going through the cloud chamber, if you are given the relevant physical theory. But there is an important apparent difference between the two cases. In the scientific case, your making that observation is itself evidence for the physical theory because the physical theory explains the proton, which explains the trail, which explains your observation. In the moral case, your making your observation does not seem to be evidence for the relevant moral principle because that principle does not seem to help explain your observation. The explanatory chain from principle to observation seems to be broken in morality. The moral principle may "explain" why it is wrong for the children to set the cat on fire. But the wrongness of that act does not appear to help explain the act, which you observe, itself. The explanatory chain appears to be broken in such a way that neither the moral principle nor the wrongness of the act can help explain why you observe what you observe.

A qualification may seem to be needed here. Perhaps the children perversely set the cat on fire simply "because it is wrong." Here it may seem at first that the actual wrongness of the act does help explain why they do it and therefore indirectly helps explain why you observe what you observe just as a physical theory, by explaining why the proton is producing a vapor trail, indirectly helps explain why the observer observes what he observes. But on reflection we must agree that this is probably an illusion. What explains the children's act is not clearly the actual wrongness of the act but, rather, their belief that the act is wrong. The actual rightness or wrongness of their act seems to have nothing to do with why they do it.

Observational evidence plays a part in science it does not appear to play in ethics, because scientific principles can be justified ultimately by their role in explaining observations, in the second sense of observation—by their explanatory role. Apparently, moral principles cannot be justified in the same way. It appears to be true that there can be no explanatory chain between moral principles and particular observings in the way that there can be such a chain between scientific principles and particular observings. Conceived as an explanatory theory, morality, unlike science, seems to be cut off from observation.

Not that every legitimate scientific hypothesis is susceptible to direct observational testing. Certain hypothesis about "black holes" in space cannot be directly tested, for example, because no signal is emitted from within a black hole. The connection with observation in such a case is indirect. And there are many similar examples. Nevertheless, seen in the large, there is the apparent difference between science and ethics we have noted. The scientific realm is accessible to observation in a way the moral realm is not.

4. Ethics and mathematics

Perhaps ethics is to be compared, not with physics, but with mathematics. Perhaps such a moral principle as "You ought to keep your promises" is confirmed or disconfirmed in the way (whatever it is) in which such a mathematical principle as "5 + 7 = 12" is. Observation does not seem to play the role in mathematics it plays in physics. We do not and cannot perceive numbers, for example, since we cannot be in causal contact with them. We do not even understand what it would be like to be in causal contact with the number 12, say. Relations among numbers cannot have any more of an effect on our perceptual apparatus than moral facts can.

Observation, however, *is* relevant to mathematics. In explaining the observations that support a physical theory, scientists typically appeal to mathematical principles. On the other hand, one never seems to need to appeal in this way to moral principles. Since an observation is evidence for what best explains it, and since mathematics often figures in the explanations of scientific observations, there is indirect observational evidence for mathematics. There does not seem to be observational evidence, even indirectly, for basic moral principles. In explaining why certain observations have been made, we never seem to use purely moral assumptions. In this respect, then, ethics appears to differ not only from physics but also from mathematics.

In what follows, we will be considering a number of possible responses to the apparent fact that ethics is cut off from observational testing in a way that science is not. Some of these responses claim that there is a distinction of this sort between science and ethics and try to say what its implications are. Others deny that there is a distinction of this sort between science and ethics and argue that ethics is not really exempt from observational testing in the way it appears to be.

A note on further reading

For a brief argument distinguishing the role of observational evidence in ethics and in science, see R. M. Hare, *Freedom and Reason* (Oxford, Oxford University Press, 1963), pp. 1–3.

Alan Gewirth notes some complications in "Positive 'Ethics' and Normative 'Science'," *Philosophical Review*, Vol. 69 (1960).

On the "theory of ladenness" of observation, see Norwood Russell Hanson, *Patterns of Discovery* (Cambridge, Cambridge University Press, 1958), Chapter 1.

The role of explanation in inference is discussed in Gilbert Harman, "Inference to the Best Explanation," *Philosophical Review*, Vol. 74 (1965).

The suggestions that there can be intuitive knowledge of moral truths is examined in P. F. Strawson, "Ethical Intuitionism," *Philosophy*, Vol. 24 (1949).

Paul Benacerraf discusses problems about mathematical knowledge in "Mathematical Truth," *Journal of Philosophy*, Vol. 70 (1973).

2 Nihilism and naturalism

1. Moral nihilism

We have seen that observational evidence plays a role in science and mathematics it does not seem to play in ethics. Moral hypotheses do not help explain why people observe what they observe. So ethics is problematic and nihilism must be taken seriously. Nihilism is the doctrine that there are no moral facts, no moral truths, and no moral knowledge. This doctrine can account for why reference to moral facts does not seem to help explain observations, on the grounds that what does not exist cannot explain anything.

An extreme version of nihilism holds that morality is simply an illusion: nothing is ever right or wrong, just or unjust, good or bad. In this version, we should abandon morality, just as an atheist abandons religion after he has decided that religious facts cannot help explain observations. Some extreme nihilists have even suggested that morality is merely a superstitious remnant of religion.

Such extreme nihilism is hard to accept. It implies that there are no moral constraints—that everything is permitted. As Dostoevsky observes, it implies that there is nothing wrong with murdering your father. It also implies that slavery is not unjust and that Hitler's extermination camps were not immoral. These are not easy conclusions to accept.

This, of course, does not refute extreme nihilism. Nihilism does not purport to reflect our ordinary views; and the fact that it is difficult to believe does not mean that it must be false. At one time in the history of the world people had difficulty in believing that the earth was round; nevertheless the earth was round. A truly religious person could not easily come to believe that God does not exist; that is no argument against atheism. Extreme nihilism is a possible view and it deserves to be taken seriously.

On the other hand, it is also worth pointing out that extreme nihilism is not an automatic consequence of the point that moral facts apparently cannot help explain observations. Although this is grounds for nihilism, there are more moderate versions of nihilism. Not all versions imply that morality is a delusion and that moral judgments are to be abandoned the way an atheist abandons religious judgments. Thus, a more moderate nihilism holds that the purpose of moral judgments is not to describe the world but to express our moral feelings or to serve as imperatives we address to ourselves and to others. In this view, morality is not undermined by its apparent failure to explain observations, because to expect moral judgments to be of help in explaining observations is to be confused about the function of morality. It is as if you were to expect to explain observations by exclaiming, "Alas!" or by commanding, "Close the door!"

Moderate nihilism is easier to accept than extreme nihilism. It allows us to keep morality and continue to make moral judgments. It does not imply that there is nothing wrong with murdering your father, owning slaves, or setting up extermination camps. Because we disapprove of these activities, we can, according to moderate nihilism, legitimately express our disapproval by saying that they are wrong.

Moderate nihilism, nevertheless, still conflicts with common sense, even if the conflict is less blatant. To assert, as even moderate nihilists assert, that there are no moral facts, no moral truths, and no moral knowledge is to assert something that runs counter to much that we ordinarily think and say. If someone suggests that it was wrong of members of the Oregon Taxpayers Union to have kidnapped Sally Jones in order to get at her father, Austin P. Jones, and you agree, you will express your agreement by saying, "That's *true!*" Similarly, in deciding what to do on a particular occasion, you say such things as this, "I *know* that I should not break my promise to Herbert, but I really would like to go to the beach today." We ordinarily do speak of moral judgments as true or false; and we talk as if we knew certain moral truths but not others.

Nihilism, then, extreme or moderate, is in conflict with ordinary ways of talking and thinking. Although such a conflict does not refute a theory, we must ask whether we can accommodate the point about ethics and observation without having to give up our ordinary views and endorsing some form of nihilism.

2. Reductions

Our previous discussion suggests the following argument for moral nihilism:

> Moral hypotheses never help explain why we observe anything. So we have no evidence for our moral opinions.

The argument depends upon this assumption:

> We can have evidence for hypotheses of a certain sort only if such hypotheses sometimes help explain why we observe what we observe.

But that assumption is too strong. Hypotheses about the average American citizen never help explain why we observe anything about a particular American, but we can obtain evidence for such hypotheses by obtaining evidence for hypotheses about American citizens. The reason is that facts about the average American citizen are definable in terms of facts about American citizens. Facts of the first sort are constructed out of and therefore reducible to facts of the second sort. Even if assumptions about moral facts do not directly help explain observations, it may be that moral facts can be reduced to other sorts of facts and that assumptions about these facts do help explain observations. In that case, there could be evidence for assumptions about moral facts.

To take another example, we might be able to account for color perception without making the supposition that objects actually have colors. For we might be able to explain how objects whose surfaces have certain physical characteristics will reflect light of a particular wave length; this light then strikes the retina of an observer's eye, affecting him in a way that might be described by an adequate neurophysiological psychology. That is, we might be able to explain perception of color entirely in terms of the physical characteristics of the objects perceived and the properties of light together with an account of the perceptual apparatus of the observer. This would not prove that there are no facts about colors; it would only show that facts about colors are not additional facts, over and above physical and psychological facts. If we could explain color perception in this way, we would conclude that facts about color are somehow reducible to facts about the physical characteristics of perceived objects, facts about light, and facts about the psychology and perceptual apparatus of perceivers. We might consider whether moral facts are in a similar way constructible out of or reducible to certain other facts that can help explain our observations.

3. Ethical naturalism: Functionalism

This is certainly a plausible suggestion for certain nonmoral evaluative facts. Consider, for example, what is involved in something's being a good thing of its kind, a good knife, a good watch, or a good heart. Associated with these kinds of things are certain functions. A knife is something that is used for cutting; a watch is used to keep time; a heart is that organ that pumps the blood. Furthermore, something is a good thing of the relevant kind to the extent that it adequately fulfills its proper function. A good knife cuts well; a good watch keeps accurate time; a good heart pumps blood at the right pressure without faltering. Let us use the letter "K" to stand for a kind of thing. Then, for these cases, a good K is a K that adequately fulfills its function. It is a factual question whether or not something is a good K because it is a factual question whether or not K's have that function and a factual question whether or not this given something adequately fulfills that function.

Moreover, a K ought to fulfill its function. If it does not do so, something has gone wrong. Therefore, it is a factual question whether a given K of this sort is as it ought to be and does what it ought to do, and it is a factual question whether anything is wrong with a K of this sort. A knife ought to be sharp, so that it will cut well. There is something wrong with a heart that fails to pump blood without faltering.

There are, of course, two somewhat different cases here, artifacts, such as watches and knives, and parts of natural systems, such as hearts. The functions of artifacts are determined by their makers and users. The functions of parts of natural systems are determined by their roles in sustaining those systems. In either case, though, it is a factual question what the relevant function of a K is.

Let us next consider a somewhat different range of cases: a good meal, a good swim, a good time. We might stretch a point and say that meals, swims, and times have functions or purposes; but it would be more accurate to say that they can answer to certain interests. We judge that particular meals, swims, or times are good inasmuch as they answer to the relevant interests. Where different sets of interests are relevant, we get ambiguity: "a good meal" may mean a nourishing meal or a tasty meal.

With this range of cases, "ought" and "wrong" are used as before. A good meal ought to be balanced (or tasty.). There is something wrong with a steak that is not tender and juicy.

More complex cases involve roles that a person can have in one way or another: a good farmer, a good soldier, a good teacher, a good citizen, a good thief. A person is evaluated in terms of functions, roles, and various interests in a way that is hard to specify. Here too the words "ought" and "wrong" are relevant as before. During battle, we say, a soldier ought to obey his superior officers without question. It is wrong for a teacher to play favorites. A thief ought to wear gloves.

Some kinds of things are not associated with functions, purposes, or sets of interests; for example, rocks per se are not. Therefore, it does not make sense to ask apart from a specific context whether something is a good rock. We can answer such a question only in relation to interests that we might have in possible uses of the rock. For example, it might be a good rock to use as a paperweight; but, if it is to be used as a doorstop, maybe it ought to be heavier.

The relevant evaluative judgments are factual. The facts are natural facts though somewhat complex facts. We judge that something is good or bad, that it is right or wrong, that it ought or ought not to have certain characteristics or do certain things, relative to a cluster of interests, roles, and functions. We can abbreviate this by saying that something X is good to the extent that it adequately answers to the relevant interests. To specify those interests is to specify what X is good as. Similarly, a person P ought to do D if and only if P's doing D would answer to the relevant interests.

This analysis is a realistic one for many cases and it suggests how evaluative facts might be constructed out of observable facts even when the evaluative facts themselves do not figure in explanations of observations. That my watch is a good one may not explain anything about my observations of it; but that it keeps fairly accurate time does help to explain its continual agreement with the announcements of the time on the radio and perhaps the goodness of my watch consists in facts of this sort.

But a problem manifests itself when this sort of analysis is applied in ethics. Consider the case in which you are a doctor who either can save five patients by cutting up the healthy patient in Room 306 and distributing his organs to the other patients or can do nothing and let the five other patients die. The problem is that in either case you would be satisfying certain interests and not others. The interests of the five dying patients conflict with the interests of the healthy patient in Room 306. The moral question is what you ought to do, taking all interests into account. As we saw earlier, our intuitive judgment is that you ought not to sacrifice the one patient in Room 306 to save the five other patients. Is this a factual judgment? If we suppose that it is a fact that you ought not to sacrifice the patient in Room 306, how is that fact related to facts that can help explain observations? It is not at all obvious how we can extend our analysis to cover this sort of case.

Actually, the problem is not peculiar to ethics. Is a heavy, waterproof, shockproof watch that can withstand a considerable amount of pressure a better or worse watch than a lighter, graceful, delicate watch without those features? Is one teacher better or worse than a second if the first teacher makes students unhappy while teaching them more?

To some extent, our difficulty in these cases lies in the vagueness of our standards for watches and teachers. Often we can resolve the vagueness by specifying relevant interests. The heavy watch is a better watch for deep-sea diving. The lighter watch is better for social occasions, out of the water. In the case of evaluating teachers, we must decide what we want from teachers—perhaps that their students should learn a certain minimal amount and, given that they learn at least that much, that they not be made miserable. But even given further specifications of our interests in watches and teachers in this way, there may be no fact of the matter as to which watch or teacher is better—not because these are not factual questions but because of vagueness of standards. Factual questions are still factual even when they cannot be answered because of vagueness. (Is a door open or shut if it is slightly ajar?) Furthermore, even in cases where we feel intuitively that one watch or teacher is clearly better, we may not be able to specify very clearly the interests, functions, and roles with reference to which one is better, as a watch or teacher, than the other. Still, it may well be a fact that one is better—a fact constructed in a way that we can only vaguely specify from facts of a sort that can help explain observations.

Similarly, it *may* be that moral facts, such as the fact that you ought not to sacrifice the healthy patient in Room 306 to save the five other patients, can be constructed in some way or other out of facts of a sort that can explain observations, even though we can only vaguely indicate relevant roles, interests, and functions.

That would vindicate ethical naturalism, which is the doctrine that moral facts are facts of nature. Naturalism as a general view is the sensible thesis that *all* facts are facts of nature. Of course, one can accept naturalism in general without being committed to ethical naturalism, since one can instead be a nihilist and deny that there are any moral facts at all, just as one might deny that there are any religious facts. Naturalists must be either ethical nihilists or ethical naturalists. The question is how do we decide between ethical nihilism and ethical naturalism, and there is no simple answer. If an analysis of moral facts as facts about functions, roles, and interests could be made plausible, that would be a powerful argument for ethical naturalism. But the relevant functions, roles, and interests can at best be only vaguely indicated, so the proposed analysis is difficult to evaluate. Nihilism remains a possibility.

4. The open question argument

On the other hand, general arguments against ethical naturalism, and for nihilism, are also inconclusive. For example, moderate nihilists argue that naturalists misconstrue the function of moral

judgments, which is not to describe the facts (they say) but
rather to express the speaker's approval or disapproval. Therefore, moderate nihilists say that ethical naturalism involves a
"naturalistic fallacy." But as we shall see, the evaluation of this
moderate nihilist position is also quite complex.

An ethical naturalist holds that there are moral facts and that
these can be "reduced" to natural facts of a sort that might
explain observations in the way that facts about color might be
reduced to facts about physical characteristics of objects, the
properties of light, and the perceptual apparatus of an observer.
I have alluded to one way in which an ethical naturalist might
attempt such a reduction by appealing to functions, roles, and
interests. There are also other ways; he might, for example, try to
develop an "ideal observer" theory of moral facts by analogy
with the suggested theory of color facts. We will be considering
just such an ideal observer theory later, in Chapter 4. And other
kinds of ethical naturalism are also possible. Now, some moderate nihilists believe that there is a perfectly general argument
that can be used once and for all to show that any version of
ethical naturalism must fail. This is the so-called "open question
argument." Any naturalistic reduction in ethics would have the
form, "P ought to do D if and only if P's doing D has characteristics C," in which the characteristics C are naturalistic characteristics of a sort that can help explain observations. Given any
such proposed naturalistic reduction, defenders of the open
question argument maintain that the following question remains
open.

> I agree that for P to do D would be for P to do some-
> thing that is C, but ought P to do D?

This remains an open question, moderate nihilists say, because
describing an act is not the same as endorsing it. No matter how
you describe it, you have so far not endorsed it and, therefore,
have not yet said whether it ought to be done, according to
moderate nihilists. Therefore, the displayed question is (they
assert) an open question in a way that the following question is
not.

> I agree that P ought to do D, but ought P to do D?

This question is obviously foolish. Given that something ought to
be done, it cannot be an open question whether it ought to be

done. And since the first question is an open question but the second is not, we are to conclude that the natural characteristic of being an act that is C cannot be equated with the moral characteristic of being an act that ought to be done.

One problem with this argument is that it has to be shown that the first question is always open. An ethical nihilist is simply begging the question if he only says, in arguing against ethical naturalism, that describing an act as having certain natural characteristics cannot amount to endorsing the act in the sense of saying that it ought to be done. It is not obvious, for example, that the following question is open in the relevant sense.

> I agree that, if P does D, P will satisfy the relevant interests, but ought P to do D?

Of course, one part of the problem here is that the "relevant interests" are not specified in a precise naturalistic way. Nevertheless, it is not obvious that, if they are so specified, the question is open.

More important, perhaps, is the fact that as it stands the open question argument is invalid. An analogous argument could be used on someone who was ignorant of the chemical composition of water to "prove" to him that water is not H_2O. This person will agree that it is not an open question whether water is water but it is an open question, at least for him, whether water is H_2O. Since this argument would not show that water is not H_2O, the open question argument in ethics cannot be used as it stands to show that for an act to be an act that ought to be done is not for it to have some natural characteristic C.

The open question argument is often put forward as a refutation, not of ethical naturalism in general, but of a more particular version, which we might call definitional naturalism. Definitional naturalists assume that moral judgments are definitionally equivalent to natural judgments. The open question argument then should show that the proposed definitions must be incorrect.

There are, however, various kinds of definitions and the open question argument is not relevant to most of them. For example, a scientist defines water as H_2O and, as we have seen, the open question argument applied to this definition does not refute it.

Presumably the open question argument is aimed at someone

who claims that a naturalistic definition captures the meaning of a moral term in the sense that moral judgments as we ordinarily use them are synonymous with judgments that describe natural facts. If it really is an open question whether an act that is C is an act that ought to be done—an open question even to someone who knows the meanings of "C" and "ought to be done," how can "C" and "ought to be done" be synonymous? It must be shown, not just assumed, however, that the relevant question is always open, no matter what the natural characteristics C.

Redefinitional naturalism

Another kind of definitional naturalism in ethics is actually not a version of ethical naturalism at all. In this view, our moral terminology is so vague, unclear, and confused that we would do well to replace it with better and more precise terminology. For example, someone who was developing the theory that you ought to do what answers to the relevant interests might argue that our view about the example involving the patient in Room 306 shows that our moral views are incoherent. He might go on to suggest that we replace our present notions with clearer concepts, for example, defining "ought" so that an act ought to be done if and only if it would maximize the satisfaction of interests. By this utilitarian criterion, you ought to cut up the patient in Room 306 in order to save the other patients. It is true that the proposed definition does not capture the ordinary meaning of "ought," since, when we judge intuitively that you ought to protect the healthy patient in Room 306, we are definitely not judging that this would maximize the satisfaction of interests—indeed we see that it would not. But a definition need not capture what we ordinarily mean. We can define our terms however we like, as long as we are willing to use these terms in accordance with our definitions. The suggested definition is relatively clear and precise. What is a better definition?

This line of argument is intelligible and not absurd, although it is also not without its own difficulties. It must be shown and not just assumed that ordinary moral notions are confused. This is a debatable claim. The fact that there is no obvious way to define ordinary moral terminology in a precise way does not show that there is anything wrong with that terminology. Not every term can be defined; it may be that moral terminology cannot be reduced to any simpler terminology.

Furthermore, there is a risk in this line of argument in that someone who takes this line may cheat, using "ought" sometimes as he has defined it and at other times in its ordinary sense. The best way to avoid this problem would be to dispense altogether with moral terminology in favor of utilitarian terminology and, instead of talking about what people ought to do, talk instead about what would satisfy the most interests. But that would be to give up any pretense of ethical naturalism and reveal that you have adopted extreme nihilism. It would involve denying that there are moral facts in the ordinary sense of "moral" and would ask us to abandon morality in the ordinary sense of "morality," just as a general naturalist abandons religion in the ordinary sense of "religion."

6. Why ethics is problematic

Although we are in no position to assume that nihilism, extreme or moderate, is correct, we are now in a position to see more clearly the way in which ethics is problematic. Our starting point in this chapter was that moral judgments do not seem to help explain observations. This led us to wonder whether there are moral facts, moral truths, and moral knowledge. We saw that there could be moral facts if these facts were reducible in some way or other to other facts of a sort that might help explain observations. For we noticed that there are facts about the average American citizen, even though such facts do not themselves help explain observations, because such facts are reducible to facts about American citizens that can help explain observations. Similarly, we noticed that we would not decide that there are no facts about colors even if we were able to explain color perception without appealing to facts about colors; we would instead suppose that facts about colors are reducible to facts about the physical surfaces of objects, the properties of light, and the neurophysiological psychology of observers. So, we concluded that we did not have to accept ethical nihilism simply because moral facts do not seem to help explain observations; instead we might hope for a naturalistic reduction of moral facts.

With this in mind, we considered the possibility that moral facts might be reduced to facts about interests, roles, and functions. We concluded that, if they were to be, the reduction would have to be complex, vague, and difficult to specify. Ethics remains problematic.

It is true that the reduction of facts about colors is also complex, vague, and difficult (probably impossible) to specify. But there is an important difference between facts about colors and moral facts. Even if we come to be able to explain color perception by appeal to the physical characteristics of surfaces, the properties of light, and the neurophysiological psychology of observers, we will still *sometimes* refer to the actual colors of objects in explaining color perception, if only for the sake of simplicity. For example, we will explain that something looks green because it is yellow and the light is blue. It may be that the reference to the actual color of the object in an explanation of this sort can be replaced with talk about the physical characteristics of the surface. But that would greatly complicate what is a simple and easily understood explanation. That is why, even after we come to be able to give explanations without referring to the actual colors of objects, we will still assume that objects have actual colors and that therefore facts about the actual colors of objects are somehow reducible to facts about physical characteristics of surfaces and so forth, even though we will (probably) not be able to specify the reduction in any but the vaguest way. We will continue to believe that objects have colors because we will continue to refer to the actual colors of objects in the explanations that we will in practice give. A similar point does not seem to hold for moral facts. There does not ever seem to be, even in practice, any point to explaining someone's moral observations by appeal to what is actually right or wrong, just or unjust, good or bad. It always seems to be more accurate to explain moral observations by citing facts about moral views, moral sensibility. So, the reasons we have for supposing that there are facts about colors do not correspond to reasons for thinking that there are moral facts.

It is true that facts about the average American citizen never seem to help explain observations, even in practice. In this respect such facts are like moral facts. But there is this difference. We can give a *precise* reduction of facts about the average American citizen; we cannot for moral facts. We are willing to think that there are facts about the average American citizen because we can explicitly define these facts in terms of facts that are of a sort that can help to explain observations. The trouble with alleged moral facts is that, as far as we can see at present, there is no simple and precise way to define them in terms of natural facts.

We are willing to suppose that there are facts about color, despite our not knowing precisely how to reduce them, because in practice we assume that there are such facts in many of our explanations of color perception, even if in theory this assumption is dispensable. We are willing to suppose that there are facts about the average American citizen, despite our never using such an assumption to explain observations, because we can precisely reduce these facts to facts of a sort that can help explain observations. Since moral facts seem to be neither precisely reducible nor useful even in practice in our explanations of observations, it remains problematic whether we have any reason to suppose that there are any moral facts.

A note on further reading

Fyodor Dostoevsky examines the implications of moral nihilism in his novels, *Crime and Punishment* and *The Brothers Karamazov*.

Friedrich Nietzsche argues that there are no moral facts and that morality as it has existed until now must be rejected in *Twilight of the Idols* in *The Portable Nietzsche*, edited and translated by Walter Kaufmann (New York: Viking Press, 1954).

A. J. Ayer argues that moral statements have no "cognitive meaning" in *Language, Truth, and Logic* (New York: Dover, 1950).

For discussion of the idea that the word "good" might be characterized in functional terms, see Philippa Foot, "Goodness and Choice," *Proceedings of the Aristotelian Society*, Supplementary volume 25 (1961), and Jerrold J. Katz, "Semantic Theory and the Meaning of 'Good,'" *Journal of Philosophy*, Vol. 61 (1964).

On the "naturalistic fallacy," see G. E. Moore, *Principia Ethica* (Cambridge: Cambridge University Press, 1903), pp. 6-21, and William K. Frankena, "The Naturalistic Fallacy," *Mind*, Vol. 48 (1939).

II
Emotivism

3 Emotivism as moderate nihilism

1. Emotivism: The basic idea

Nihilism is the doctrine that there are no moral facts, no moral truths, no moral knowledge. Moderate nihilism says that nihilism is no reason to abandon morality, since morality does not describe facts but does something else. One often made suggestion is that moral judgments express the feelings or attitudes of people making those judgments.

When you look at a moral disagreement you can see what suggests that moral judgments are merely expressions of attitudes. If I say that the Oregon Taxpayers Union was right to kidnap Sally Jones and you say that it was wrong, you and I are disagreeing. Among other things, we disagree in our attitude toward the kidnapping. I favor it and you are against it. I have a pro-attitude toward the kidnapping and you have a con-attitude. We may or may not differ in our beliefs about the Oregon Taxpayers Union, what they did, who Sally Jones is, who her father, Austin P. Jones; is, and so forth. But whether or not we differ in belief, we also disagree in attitude, and our moral disagreement, concerning whether it was right or wrong for the Oregon Taxpayers Union to kidnap Sally Jones, is this disagreement in attitude. No matter what beliefs about the facts we come to agree on, as long as we disagree in attitude our moral disagreement persists. And, as soon as we agree in attitude, our moral disagreement has ended, no matter what difference in belief remains.

You might say then that "X is wrong" means "I disapprove of X." But that would not be a correct formulation. My moral judgment is not *about* my approval or disapproval; rather it *expresses* my approval or disapproval. My moral judgment is to my moral approval as my factual judgment is to my belief. If I say that Sally Jones was a sophomore in college at the time that she was kidnapped and you say that she was a junior, our disagreement is a disagreement in belief—but we are not talking *about* our beliefs, we are expressing them. The remark, "Sally Jones was a sophomore" is not equivalent to the remark, "One of my beliefs is that Sally Jones was a sophomore." But the remark, "Sally Jones was a sophomore" expresses the belief that Sally Jones was a sophomore. Similarly, if I remark that the Oregon Taxpayers Union was right to have kidnapped Sally Jones, what I say is not equivalent to *saying that* I approve of the Union having done that, but it does express my approval of the kidnapping.

The view we have been discussing is often called "emotivism" —moral judgments express the speaker's emotions, feelings, attitudes, intentions, or more generally, norms and values. For to value something is not just to have a belief about something; it is to have an attitude toward something. It is to be in favor of something. To value something is to be in an emotional state, not a cognitive state.

Emotivism may at first appear to be a radical and controversial theory. But when it has been fully elaborated and when objections have been disposed of, we shall see that it has become a tamer view than it seemed at the beginning.

Notice, for one thing, that emotivism is a version of what we earlier called moderate nihilism. It holds that there are no moral facts; but it does not conclude that moral terminology is confused and dispensible in the way that religious terminology is, according to an atheist. People are in favor of some things and against other things and what they are in favor of and against has a bearing on what they decide to do. A practical decision requires a kind of practical reasoning that is not simply reasoning about what to believe but is concerned with what to do. Moral terminology is needed to express the considerations that are relevant to practical reasoning and argument.

2. Emotivism and the open question argument

Emotivists often invoke the open question argument against ethical naturalists. The emotivist is inclined to suppose that it will always be an open question whether something that has any given natural characteristic is wrong, because the emotivist believes that the word "wrong" carries an emotive force that a descriptive expression like "causes human suffering" must lack. No matter what natural characteristic C is, the emotivist is inclined to argue, to believe that something is C is not yet to have an attitude of disapproval, whereas to think that something is wrong is already to be against it. To agree that something is C is, so far, to leave it open whether you think that it is wrong, the emotivist argues.

Although emotivists often use the open question argument in this way, they rely on something that goes beyond the basic principles of emotivism. There is also a hidden assumption here that must be brought into the open, namely the assumption that values are not universal. For suppose that values are universal. In particular, suppose that whenever anyone believes that an action causes human suffering, he immediately disapproves of it. Then the open question argument fails. For then, to believe that an action causes human suffering is automatically to disapprove of it and therefore, given emotivism, to believe that it is wrong. The question whether an action that causes human suffering is wrong is no longer an open question. The gap between "causes human suffering" and "is wrong" is closed.

It is compatible with emotivism to say that there are universal values. Such values might be innate, "wired in" genetically by virtue of evolution. People born without built-in values of sociability and self-preservation may have lost out in the evolutionary competition to others who were born with such values. The Scottish philosopher David Hume (1711--1776) argues that people are so constructed that they feel a certain weak sympathy for other people. According to Hume, as long as your own interests are not at stake, you will automatically be in favor of what is for the good of other people. If Hume is right, it cannot be an open question whether or not you favor doing something that will benefit some people and harm no one. For to think that something would accomplish this is to be in favor of it, according to Hume, and that would be to think that it was a good thing, according to emotivism.

If emotivism is accepted, the extent to which there is a gap between is and ought becomes the psychological question, "What values are part of human nature?" It is conceivable that, given human nature as it is, moral thinking always relies upon certain basic universal values. If this is true, emotivism can be conjoined with a highly nonskeptical and nonrelativistic ethical theory. On the other hand, it is also possible that human nature is more variable and that different people have different values and principles and this variation does not have to involve irrationality. If so, emotivism becomes a more skeptical, more relativistic ethical theory.

Emotivism says that moral judgments express attitudes for and against things. This can be part of a nonrelativistic theory if it is combined with the view that there is a uniformity in basic human attitudes. If emotivism is combined with the view that there is no such uniformity, it becomes part of a more relativistic theory. But the relativism derives not so much from the emotivism as from the view taken of human nature.

This means that emotivism is not, by itself, a version of nihilism. It is compatible with emotivism to assume that there are moral facts, if you also assume that there is enough uniformity in human nature. An emotivist can even be an ethical naturalist. For example, if an emotivist believes that moral approval and disapproval derives from a universal sympathy we feel for others, then he might adopt a naturalistic definition of moral wrongness—X is wrong to the extent that X causes human suffering. The open question argument would present no obstacle to this definition, since such an emotivist will hold that, because of universal sympathy, it cannot be an open question whether something that causes human suffering is to that extent wrong. Hume has been interpreted, in this way, as both an emotivist and an ethical naturalist.

A difference between emotivism and ethical naturalism emerges only if a different view is taken of human nature. For example, suppose that human nature imposes no real constraints on basic values and that practical reasoning creates no new values but only enables you to pursue your values in the light of whatever information you have. Suppose, then, that there are no universal values it is irrational not to have. In other words, suppose that practical reason always is and ought to be the slave of the passions. This would be to accept the sort of conception of practical reasoning we find in Aristotle (384–322 B.C.) or Hume.

The idea is that you start out with certain ends—things that you favor or want. Then theoretical reasoning tells you that, in order to get one of these ends, you need something else. This might be something you can do or something that might happen. Then practical reasoning leads you to take this other thing as an intermediate end—something that you favor or want because it will lead to your original end. Practical reasoning is always means–ends reasoning of this sort, according to Hume and Aristotle; you can come to want something as a means to something else you already want. But such reasoning can have no effect on your ultimate ends. You cannot reason yourself into having something as a new ultimate end, since you always reason from your ends to things that are means to those ends.

It is not obvious that this account of practical reasoning is correct; as we shall see there are those who reject it. But it is a plausible account and, if that account of practical reasoning is accepted and if there are no interesting constraints on ultimate ends, then emotivism has to be a relativistic and skeptical theory. Emotivism cannot in that case involve ethical naturalism; indeed, emotivists will then say that the open question argument shows that there is a naturalisitic fallacy.

The ethical naturalist identifies an action's being wrong with its having some natural characteristic. He may say, for example, that for an act to be wrong is for it to cause human suffering. Now, it is true that if someone's ultimate ends are such that he is against any act that causes human suffering, he will not think that it is an open question whether an act that causes human suffering is thereby wrong. But we are now assuming for the moment that there will also be people with different ultimate ends who do not care whether acts cause human suffering. Such people will think that it is (at least) an open question whether an act that causes human suffering is thereby wrong. These people will be able to think that an act causes human suffering without disapproving of it and, since we are supposing that it is not irrational of them to fail in this way to disapprove of acts that cause human suffering, it will in fact be for them an open question whether or not an act that causes human suffering is thereby wrong. So, the ethical naturalist in question will not have captured the way in which these people use the term "wrong."

The ethical naturalist might reply that he is not trying to capture everyone's usage, only his own. He defines his terms as he does because he disapproves of acts that cause human suffering, even if there are other people who do not similarly disapprove of acts that cause human suffering. But this is unsatisfactory. The ethical naturalist's definition will not work even when he applies it to his own usage. For suppose he gets into an argument with someone who does not disapprove of acts that cause human suffering. This other person says that these things are *not wrong*. "Ah!" replies the ethical naturalist, "As I am using words, these things are wrong, since I define 'wrong' to mean 'causes human suffering.'" And of course, the ethical naturalist can use words any way he wishes. But that will not end the disagreement between him and the other person; and the ethical naturalist will want to be able to express what is at issue in their disagreement. But how? If his terminology is purely descriptive and factual, there may be no way to express the disagreement, for the two of them may agree about all relevant facts. It will not do to say that in such a case there is no real disagreement, because there is still a disagreement in attitude. Of course, the ethical naturalist can allow this disagreement in attitude to be *described*. He can say that he is against something that the other person is not against. But he cannot allow this disagreement to be *expressed* unless he allows into his language not only ways of talking *about* attitudes but ways of expressing attitudes. And once he allows himself a way of expressing attitudes, he is using terminology that cannot be defined in purely descriptive terms, given our present assumption that human nature is not so uniform that we all have the same basic values (and given that reason is the slave of the passions). Given this assumption, emotivism is therefore much more plausible than ethical naturalism.

3. Advantages of emotivism

Let me now briefly review what I have been saying. Emotivism is the theory that your moral judgments express your attitudes. In other words, your moral beliefs (if it is proper to speak of "beliefs" in this connection) are not cognitive but are themselves attitudes for or against something. According to emotivism, "I believe that this act is wrong" means roughly "I disapprove of this act." But "This act is wrong," by itself, cannot be equated with any purely naturalistic expression like "this act causes human suffering" unless there is a law of nature that to think that an act causes human suffering is to be against it—to disapprove of it.

Emotivism has a number of things in its favor. First, it gives a plausible account of moral disagreement. Such disagreement is a kind of disagreement in attitude, one person favors something, another is against it. Furthermore, certain moral disagreements are irresolvable; the parties to the disagreement can argue and argue—quite rationally and even calmly—without reaching agreement. The emotivist can explain this by assuming that the parties to the dispute have different basic values. Ultimately, they want different things and neither need be irrational or confused in wanting what he wants.

Second, emotivism accounts for the importance of moral question in our lives and for the way in which our moral beliefs are tied to our acts. To be in favor of something is to want it to happen. To be against something is to want it not to happen. And what you want influences what you do.

To think that you ought to do something is to be motivated to do it. To think that it would be wrong to do something is to be motivated not to do it. Emotivism can explain this. Naturalism could explain it, too, but only by supposing a law of nature that, say, everyone disapproves of acts that cause human suffering. The naturalistic explanation is less secure, ad hoc, and not as fundamental as the emotivist explanation, which does not assume any such law of nature.

These are the advantages of emotivism: its account of moral disagreement and its emphasis on the connection between moral beliefs and passions and acts. Now let us turn to possible objections and problems.

Truth in ethics

I mentioned one objection in the previous chapter. How can emotivism account for the fact that we sometimes call moral judgments true or false? Feelings and passions cannot be true or false; and, if certain remarks simply express feelings or passions, it is not easy to see how these remarks are true or false. It may be true that I like something, that I am in favor of it; but can by liking be true? If you say that political kidnapping is wrong, I can quite intelligibly agree with you by saying, "That's true." But suppose you simply express your feelings. You say, "Wow!" or "Oh boy!"

or "Ugh!" Then, for me to agree by saying, "That's true!" would be inappropriate. Similarly, if you were to utter the command, "Catch those kidnappers!" it would be odd for me to express my agreement with your sentiments by saying, "That's true!"

An emotivist *might* reply that for me to agree with your moral judgment by saying, "That's true!" is for me to misuse the term "true." Strictly speaking, he might say, moral judgments are neither true nor false, since they express attitudes that can be neither true nor false. Although this is one possible reply, it does run afoul of a maxim or rule of thumb for philosophers, namely that, if a philosophical theory conflicts with ordinary ways of thinking and speaking, examine the argument for that theory very closely, since something has probably gone wrong.

This is not an absolutely conclusive point. An atheist may arrive at conclusions that are in conflict with ordinary ways of thinking and speaking and nevertheless may feel, perhaps correctly, that it is the ordinary ways of thinking and speaking that are wrong rather than his theory. The same thing *might* be true of an emotivism that denies that moral judgments are ever true or false. Nevertheless, a conflict with ordinary ways of thinking and speaking may indicate that something has gone wrong so it is useful to consider an alternative line an emotivist might take.

The emotivist might agree that moral judgments can be properly said to be true or false. What this shows, he might go on to say, is that certain attitudes and feelings can be properly said to be true or false. This initially seems odd, he might continue, because we misconstrue what is involved in saying that something is true or false. We suppose that to say that something is true is to say that it corresponds to the facts. Since we do not see how feelings and attitudes can correspond to the facts, we do not see how they can be properly said to be either true or false. But that is because we have a misleading picture of truth as correspondence with the facts.

Consider a truth of arithmetic: "$2 + 2 = 4$." Does that correspond to the facts? Perhaps; But what facts? If it can be said to correspond to any fact at all, it must be the fact that $2 + 2 = 4$, if that is properly called a fact.

"Snow is white" is true if and only if that remark corresponds to the facts. In other words, that remark is true if and only if it is a fact that snow is white. "Snow is white" is true if and only if snow is white. Similarly, "$2 + 2 = 4$ is true if and only if $2 + 2 = 4$. "S" is true if and only if S. What it means to say that truth is correspondence with the facts is that all such principles hold, no matter what indicative sentence replaces S. To see this is to see what "true" means. The principle in question holds whether or not the sentence replacing "S" is used to express a factual or an arithmetical belief—it holds even if this sentence expresses a moral attitude. "Incest is wrong" is true if and only if incest is wrong.

If you say that incest is wrong and I say "That's true!" I am simply agreeing with you. I am not saying that your remark corresponds to the facts in some strong sense of "fact." I am only saying this in the weaker sense in which, when I say that it is a fact that incest is wrong, I am saying only that incest is wrong.

In other words, the emotivist can account for our tendency to use the words "true" or "false" of moral judgments by invoking a theory of truth according to which "it is true that S" means no more than "S." So perhaps there is a good reply to the first objection to emotivism.

In taking this line, the emotivist may appear to have abandoned nihilism. Nihilism, you will recall, is the doctrine that there are no moral facts, no moral truths, and no moral knowledge. What we have seen is that the emotivist can argue that, in the ordinary senses of "fact" and "true," there are moral facts and there are moral truths. But he cannot in any similar way argue that there is moral knowledge, since these "moral facts" and "moral truths" are neither of any apparent help in explaining why anyone observes what he observes nor in any obvious way reducible to facts and truths that are of help in explaining why anyone observes what he observes. He can agree that there are moral facts and moral truths, in a manner of speaking, even in the ordinary manner of speaking—he will not, however, suppose that these facts and truths are part of the order of nature in the sense that a scientific account of nature is incomplete if it leaves them out, nor will he suppose that there can be knowledge of facts of this sort. So there is a sense in which an emotivist who takes this line retains his nihilism.

But according to this the first objection to emotivism has not been completely met, since we do ordinarily think and talk as if we occasionally knew that we ought or ought not to do various things. Here, perhaps, the emotivist may have to say that our ordinary ways of talking and thinking are simply mistaken.

5. Moral reasoning

Now let us consider a second objection, one that asks whether emotivism can account for moral reasoning. There is, evidently, such a thing as moral reasoning; and we sometimes adopt a particular moral opinion—if "opinion" is the right word—in consequence of such reasoning. Furthermore, it strikes us as appropriate to ask for someone's reasons for his moral opinion. If someone says that it is a good thing that the Oregon Taxpayers Union kidnapped Sally Jones, we will ask him why he supposes that it is. It would strike us as odd if he said that he had no reasons—that's just the way he feels about it. That would strike us as odd because his saying that the kidnapping was a good thing suggests or even implies that (he thinks that) there are reasons for supposing that the kidnapping is a good thing.

Reasoning is not relevant in the same way to feelings. You do not reason yourself into liking or disliking something. It is often true that you simply like something, or dislike it, without having a reason. Of course, you may like something in certain respects and not in others. But this is not the same thing as liking it for certain reasons or as the result of argument.

There is a difference between ethics and aesthetics in this respect. There is moral reasoning in a sense in which there is not aesthetic reasoning. Not that there is nothing that might be called aesthetic reasoning, but the situation in aesthetics is different from the situation in ethics. What might be called aesthetic reasoning is really not reasoning at all, strictly speaking. It amounts to pointing to certain aspects of a work of art in order to have someone appreciate those aspects.

Something like that can go on in ethics too. You point out aspects of a situation to get someone to appreciate them more fully; in arguing for vegetarianism, for example, you might describe in detail how animals are treated before slaughter. But there is also something else in ethics—appeal to principle. There are moral principles and these play a role in moral argument. If someone makes a moral judgment, it strikes us as appropriate to ask him what the relevant principles are in a way that seems less appropriate when someone makes an aesthetic judgment. It is not appropriate to ask someone who admires a painting what his principle is. And it is not clear that the emotivist can account for the relevance of reasoning and appeal to principle for moral judgment.

The emotivist holds that moral judgments are expressions of feeling. But expressions of feeling do not depend on reasoning from general principles, nor do they require defense by appeal to principle, whereas moral judgments do depend on reasoning from general principles and do require defense by appeal to principle. Therefore, the emotivist would seem to be mistaken in treating moral judgments as expressions of feeling.

The emotivist might reply that "there are feelings and feelings." Some feelings, he might agree, are simple reactions, such as likes and dislikes. Other feelings, more properly called attitudes, he might continue, are more complex and involve principles and one's basic values. Moral beliefs cannot be identified with any feelings whatsoever—only with these more complex feelings and attitudes.

But, unless the emotivist says more than this, his view takes on an ad hoc character. For nothing has so far been said as to why certain feelings should differ from others in this way. It is obscure why a feeling or attitude is the sort of thing to which reasoning from principles could be relevant. But before we consider what more an emotivist might say about this, let us consider a third objection that reinforces the second.

You sometimes make a moral judgment that you later decide was mistaken. If your moral beliefs were simply feelings, it is not clear how they could be mistaken in this way. At one time you felt one way; now you feel another way. In what sense can you suppose that your first feeling was mistaken? Years ago you used to like sugar in your coffee; now you do not. But you would not say that you were mistaken to have once liked sugar. On the other hand, if you once thought that incest was wrong and now think that it is right, you do suppose you were mistaken before. How can this change in moral belief be simply a change in your feelings?

6. Hume's way out

Now Hume, who may or may not be an emotivist, suggests a way round both these objections. Hume points out that many feelings and passions depend on your having beliefs about the objects of the feelings. If these beliefs are seriously mistaken, you will also say that the feeling is mistaken. In other words, you transfer the word "mistaken" from the beliefs to the feelings that depend on them.

For example, you may be mistaken in having trusted someone. Your beliefs about the reliability and sentiments of that person may be mistaken. You trusted him because you had certain beliefs about him. Since those beliefs were mistaken—and since you would not have trusted him had you known the truth—you say that your trust is mistaken.

A revolutionary might be happy that the Oregon Taxpayers Union kidnapped Sally Jones because he believes that the kidnapping will eventually lead to a revitalization of the revolutionary left. If his belief is mistaken and the kidnapping revitalizes the revolutionary right, he will say that he was mistaken to be happy.

In other words, feelings are said to be or not to be mistaken with reference to beliefs, which may or may not be mistaken, on which the feelings depend. If moral feelings are the sorts of feelings, like trust and happiness, that depend on your beliefs, it will be appropriate to say that moral feelings are mistaken when the relevant beliefs are mistaken. For example, if the revolutionary had initially judged that the Jones kidnapping was a good thing, because of his beliefs about its consequences, and then came to believe that the consequences were going to be the exact opposite, he would then suppose that his initial moral judgment had been mistaken, because the beliefs on which it had been based had been mistaken.

This shows that the emotivist can account for our willingness to say that our own past moral judgments were mistaken and can therefore answer the third objection. Hume would also say that a similar answer can be given to the second objection, concerning moral principles and moral reasoning. For, if moral judgments express attitudes that depend on beliefs about facts of a certain sort, and if these beliefs involve assumptions of a general sort, then the reasoning relevant to these factual assumptions may involve general principles. And, just as we are willing to say that moral judgments are mistaken if the corresponding beliefs are— thus transferring the word "mistaken" from beliefs to the feelings that depend on them—so too we are willing to say that reasoning from general principles is relevant to morality if it is relevant to the corresponding beliefs—in this case we transfer the relevance of principled reasoning from certain beliefs to the associated feelings that depend on those beliefs.

The difference between ethics and aesthetics, according to Hume, is a difference in the relevant passions or feelings. Hume thinks that our moral feelings involve, among other things, a general sympathy for others and, consequently, our moral feelings are often based on beliefs about the general tendencies of acts to affect people's interests. We morally approve a course of action if we believe that course of action falls under principles that, if generally followed, would promote human happiness and diminish misery. This is not the only moral concern that we have, according to Hume, but it is one of them; and it is because of this concern that we suppose that moral judgment involves an appeal to general principles. The general principles in question are, in the first instance, principles about the tendency of certain courses of action, if generally adhered to, to promote happiness and diminish misery. The relevant reasoning really concerns the facts—the issue is whether or not these courses of action will in fact improve well-being. By a principle of courtesy we call this *moral* reasoning and say that the relevant principles are *moral* principles. This, then, is the way emotivism might answer the second objection.

7. The triviality of emotivism

So far we have considered three related objections to emotivism and we have seen how an emotivist might answer them. The first objection was that moral judgments are often said to be true or false; the second was that reasoning from general principles is relevant to moral judgments; the third was that we sometimes think that our moral judgments are mistaken. The emotivist might answer the first objection by appealing to a redundancy theory of truth. He might answer the second and third objections by proposing the theory that we transfer to moral judgments talk that strictly speaking applies to the factual beliefs on which the moral judgments depend.

But when emotivism is defended in this way it appears less radical than it seemed at first. For one thing, emotivism is not, even by itself, a version of ethical nihilism, since, by itself, it is compatible with ethical naturalism. It diverges from ethical naturalism only when certain assumptions are made. Furthermore, even given those assumptions, the emotivist can allow that there are moral facts and moral truths, in the ordinary sense of these terms; he can even allow that there is something properly called moral reasoning and he can agree that people can sometimes quite correctly be said to be mistaken in their moral opinions. We may begin to wonder how emotivism differs from simple common sense.

A note on further reading

Charles L. Stevenson discusses disagreement in attitude in "The Nature of Ethical Disagreement," Chapter 1 of *Facts and Values* (New Haven, Conn.: Yale University Press, 1963), pp. 1–9. See also his discussion of truth on pp. 214–20.

R. M. Hare treats moral statements as imperatives in *The Language of Morals* (Oxford: Oxford University Press, 1952). He gives a version of the open question argument against naturalism on pp. 79–93.

David Hume's writings in ethics include his *Treatise on Human Nature*, Books II and III; and *An Enquiry Concerning the Principles of Morals.*

Philippa Foot argues that emotivism and ethical naturalism are not easily distinguished in "Moral Beliefs," *Proceedings of the Aristotelian Society*, Vol. 59 (1958–1959), pp. 83–104.

On the question whether there are aesthetic principles, see Arnold Isenberg, "Critical Communication," *Philosophical Review*, Vol. 58 (1949), pp. 330–44.

4 Emotivism as the ideal observer theory

1. The ideal observer theory

Emotivism, which at first sounds like a very radical nihilistic view, can allow for moral reasoning, moral truths, and even moral facts. Emotivism is less radical and more trivial than it looks. And that is not all. As we shall see, emotivism is not easily distinguished from a version of ethical naturalism called the "ideal observer theory."

According to emotivism, moral opinions are feelings. This does not mean, however, that moral opinions cannot be correctly said to be mistaken. For feelings can be said to be mistaken if, for example, they depend on mistaken beliefs about the facts. Emotivism even allows that moral *judgments* can sometimes correctly be said to be mistaken. For a judgment that expresses a feeling can in some cases be called mistaken if the feeling expressed is mistaken.

You say, "It is a happy thing that Rudolsky was deported," expressing your happiness, which depends on your view that his deportation eliminates the last obstacle to improved East–West relations. Instead, the deportation has the opposite effect and leads to a worsening of those relations. Then, not only can it be said that you were mistaken in your happiness but also in your remark.

41

Furthermore, in saying what you say, you imply that your happiness about Rudolsky's deportation is justified and appropriate, at least from a certain point of view, given the facts; and this implication can also be ascribed to your remark. Your remark has that implication. This is connected with the fact that your remark can be called mistaken; it can be said to be mistaken because it has a false implication.

Evaluative and moral judgments are viewed in a similar way. If you say that it is a good thing that Rudolsky was deported, you imply that a certain attitude toward the deportation is justified, at least from a certain point of view. At the very least you imply that the relevant attitude does not depend on a mistaken view of the facts.

This indicates that, even if a moral judgment is simply an expression of feeling, it will involve a claim, namely the claim that the attitude expressed is appropriate and justified, at least to the extent that the attitude does not depend on a mistaken view of the facts. Indeed, the attitude itself involves that claim in the sense that you cannot simultaneously have that attitude without supposing that it is appropriate and justified. This suggests a version of ethical naturalism that takes moral judgments to involve judgments *about* feelings.

Since an attitude is appropriate and justified in the relevant sense only if it is not mistaken—in other words, only if it is not based on a mistaken view of the facts—we might try as a first approximation the following naturalistic analysis:

> X is wrong *if and only if* one would disapprove of X if one knew all the relevant facts and had no mistaken beliefs concerning the matter at hand.

We had better add immediately, "if one fully appreciated all of the facts," since an attitude can be mistaken not only by being based on false information but also by resting on an improper appreciation of the facts so that, for example, some of the facts just do not register. Our analysis therefore becomes, as a second approximation:

X is wrong *if and only if* one would disapprove of X
                                 if one knew and fully
                                 appreciated all the rele-
                                 vant facts and had no
                                 mistaken beliefs concern-
                                 ing the matter at hand.

But this is not enough. Not all disapproval is moral disapproval. In saying that something is *morally* wrong, you also
imply that your disapproval is not based solely on your own
narrow interests but also would be an appropriate attitude from
a completely disinterested and impartial point of view. You
imply that your disapproval is not derived solely from the fact
that your own interests are affected and you imply that such
disapproval would still be appropriate even if you had no
connection with the people involved. If your attitude is derived
only from your own interests and would not be sustained on an
impartial view, your attitude is unjustified and mistaken in as
much as it pretends to be a moral attitude.

Consider slave owners who approve of slavery. It is likely that
their approval rests in part on certain false beliefs about those
who are slaves. It probably rests also in part on a failure fully to
appreciate what it is like to be a slave. But, above all, it almost
certainly rests on a failure to take a disinterested view. If the
slave owners were to consider what it would be like if they
themselves were slaves, then presumably they would not feel
moral approval for slavery, even though in the actual situation
they would of course continue to be in favor of the continuing
existence of the institution from which they benefit.

Now, if the slave owners claim that slavery is morally defensible, they cannot agree that their approval of it derives
entirely from their being in an advantageous position. They
could not intelligibly defend their claim simply by saying that
they are fully are of what it is like to be a slave, but since they are
not slaves, they do not care. That is a perfectly consistent
attitude, of course, but it is not a moral attitude. The slave
owners can continue to feel moral approval of slavery only as
long as they are able to convince themselves, for example, that
slaves are better off under slavery and that an impartial observer
who knew all the facts would also approve.

Slavery is wrong, according to our present hypothesis, if and only if a disinterested impartial observer who knew all the facts and was vividly aware of and appreciated them would disapprove of slavery. The slave owners would not disapprove, but only because they were not disinterested; so their failure to disapprove would not count.

The sort of analysis we have arrived at is sometimes called an impartial spectator or ideal observer theory. According to this analysis, something is wrong if and only if an impartial spectator or ideal observer would disapprove of it; an ideal observer is defined to be disinterested, well informed, vividly aware of the relevant facts, and so forth.

If correct, this analysis yields a naturalistic reduction of moral facts. Hume, who accepts this view, compares it with the analogous theory of color, which we discussed in Chapter 2 and which says that something is red, for example, if it would look red to a normal perceiver under standard lighting conditions. In this view, colors are dispositional properties, and so are moral properties. A dispositional property is to be defined in terms of a corresponding occurrent property. For example, the dispositional property of being soluble in water is defined in terms of the occurrent property of dissolving in water. A substance is soluble in water if it would dissolve if placed in water. Similarly, an object is red if it would look red under certain conditions.

A substance can be soluble in water even though it is never placed in water. Similarly, an object can be red even when it is in a dark room. When a tree falls in the forest and there is no one there, the tree makes a loud noise, in the dispositional sense, for, if someone had been there, he would have heard a loud noise.

The occurrent property for colors is an object's looking a certain color We might speak of color sensations. An object is red if it conveys the color sensation of red to observers—just as something is warm if it gives a sensation of heat to observers. And, something is wrong if it gives "disapproval sensations" to certain observers. Wrongness is a disposition to cause disapproval.

2. Moral relativism and the ideal observer theory

We need not suppose that every ideal observer would have the same reactions. Some might disapprove of a given situation, others might be indifferent, still others might approve. How an ideal observer would react might depend on the sort of upbringing he had had. In that event, we would have to settle for a kind of moral relativism. We would have to distinguish, say, New York-wrongness, Peking-wrongness, and Moscow-wrongness, just as we now distinguish solubility in water from solubility in oil. We cannot speak simply of solubility because different substances are soluble in different liquids. Similarly, it may be that we cannot speak simply of wrongness because different things might be disapproved of by ideal observers with different upbringings. We would have to say that something was New York-wrong but not Peking-wrong if ideal observers who had been raised in New York would disapprove but not ideal observers who had been raised in Peking.

We could still say that something is simply right or wrong, if the context made it clear that only ideal observers of a given sort were relevant. For example, if all of *us* had been brought up in New York, we might say that something was simply wrong, meaning that it was New York-wrong. Similarly, when it is clear that only solubility in water is relevant we can say that a substance is soluble and be understood to mean water-soluble.

Our use of the term "fashionable" illustrates this sort of relativism. To say that something is fashionable is to say that it would look fashionable to an appropriate observer. But whether or not something will look fashionable to you will depend on the sorts of things you are used to seeing. Fashions of another age—or another place—often look quite bizarre. To say that something "is fashionable" is therefore to make a highly relativistic judgment. Thus, X is fashionable at such and such a time and place if and only if X would look fashionable to a normal fashion observer of that time and place. Moral judgments may be similarly relativistic, although not perhaps to such an extent.

The ideal observer theory need not be a relativistic theory. There is no commitment either way. In the ideal observer theory, whether relativism is true depends on the facts of human psychology. In the case of colors, for example, relativism is *not* true. Not all perceivers have the same color reactions under standard conditions, since some perceivers are colorblind. These perceivers can be classed as substandard because, first of all, their reactions are not as sensitive as those of normal perceivers (color-blind perceivers make fewer color discriminations) and, second, normal perceivers who are able to make the most discriminations do agree in their color reactions. What is true for color *might* turn out to be true for moral properties too. For it is *conceivable* that we can explain disagreements among apparently ideal moral observers by supposing that some otherwise ideal observers have a kind of moral blindness, resulting either from some sort of genetic defect or a failure in their upbringing—for example, not enough love in their earliest years. To make this claim stick it would have to be shown that this group of apparently ideal observers do not make all the moral discriminations that other ideal observers make, although the other observers make all the discriminations the first group make. Furthermore, it would have to be shown that the other ideal observers for the most part have the same moral reactions.

It is not wildly implausible that something like this might be shown. Psychological studies of the moral development of children indicate that there are a number of stages to this development, stages of increasing sophistication. Not everyone reaches the final stages of development. We might want to define rightness and wrongness only in terms of the reactions of those who have reached the highest stage of moral development, treating others as possessing a kind of moral blindness or some other deficiency.

3. Emotivism versus the ideal observer theory

This, then, is the ideal observer theory. We arrived at the theory by way of emotivism. Emotivism, which purports to be a version of moderate nihilism, leads to the ideal observer theory, which is a version of ethical naturalism. For emotivism says that moral judgments express attitudes; and, in expressing the relevant kind of attitude, a speaker implies that the attitude is appropriate and justified, at least from a certain point of view.

It is a subtle question whether this implication is an implication of what you say or only an implication of your having said it. Compare an analogous case. When you say that Rudolsky was deported, you imply that the belief that Rudolsky was deported is justified; but you do not *say* that this belief is justified, nor does *what you say* imply this, although *your saying it* does. Similarly, even though in making a moral judgment you imply that a certain attitude is justified, it does not follow that we can analyze your judgment as *saying* that that attitude is justified.

There are two possibilities. The ideal observer theory can be treated as an analysis of what you are saying when you make a moral judgment, or it can be treated as an analysis of something that you imply in making the judgment. These possibilities are not easily distinguished in practice, although they are distinguishable in theory.

There is an ultimately inconclusive argument for supposing that the ideal observer theory is an analysis of what you are saying and not just an analysis of something that you imply in making a moral judgment. The argument can be seen as an argument against emotivism, challenging the idea that moral judgments simply express attitudes for or against something. The argument is that the relation between your moral judgments and what you are for or against is more indirect than emotivism can allow. You can think that you ought to do something without wanting to do it. Indeed, this is the heart of a certain sort of moral difficulty: realizing that you should do something you do not want to do. Similarly, you may realize that someone else ought to do something that you hope he will not do. In general, there are many cases in which what you are in favor of differs from what you think ought to be the case. Therefore, emotivists are mistaken (so the argument continues) when they simply identify the thought that something ought to be the case with being in favor of it. The ideal observer theory, conceived as a theory about the *content* of a moral judgment, can easily explain these recalcitrant facts. For you can believe that under conditions of impartiality you would have a particular attitude even though you do not have that attitude now under current conditions. Analogously, you easily make moral judgments about hypothetical situations. But what do you care about what happens in a hypothetical situation? Perhaps it is true that, if the doctor *were* to cut up the patient in Room 306 and were to distribute his organs to the five dying patients, you *would* disapprove of his doing so. Emotivism is not the theory that something is wrong if, under certain conditions, you *would* disapprove of it. That is the ideal observer theory, taken as an analysis of what a moral judgment says. According to emotivism, when I now say that the doctor would be wrong, I am now expressing my present disapproval of that hypothetical act. But what could this mean?

Although this may seem to be a powerful objection to emotivism; it can be met as easily as earlier objections by invoking the strategy of "there are feelings and feelings." The emotivist will say that, when you think you ought to do something but do not want to do it, you favor doing it but also favor not doing it; you have a moral attitude in favor of doing it and a stronger but nonmoral attitude in favor of not doing it. Similarly, if you think that you ought to do something but just don't care, the emotivist will say that you care and don't care. Your moral attitude favors your doing the thing in question, but that attitude is weak and therefore overcome by your general inertia. As for hypothetical cases, the emotivist will hold that you care morally about these cases even if you do not care in some other sense. By thus distinguishing moral attitudes from other attitudes, the emotivist can meet the objection and therefore undercut the preceding argument for taking the ideal observer theory as an analysis of what you say when you make a moral judgment.

4. The threat of circularity

This response, however, represents another step in the trivialization of emotivism. The emotivist might as well take a further step and simply *stipulate* that moral beliefs are attitudes. In other words, he might as well simply count your belief that something is morally right as your being morally in favor of it: you are in favor of it at least to the extent that you think that it ought to be done. In this way he can almost make emotivism true by definition.

This is possible because the word "attitude" in English is so vague. Beliefs can be said to be attitudes. For example, your attitude toward war might be that you think that it will not happen for a couple of months. There is a sense then in which moral beliefs are, trivially, attitudes. They are attitudes in the same sense in which any belief is an attitude.

If we agree simply to stipulate that to believe that something is wrong is one way to be against it, then emotivism can hardly be distinguished from the trivial view that to say that something is wrong is to express the belief that it is wrong. Emotivism almost becomes the empty theory that the belief that something is wrong is the belief that it is wrong.

Emotivism is therefore threatened with triviality, unless some noncircular way of identifying moral attitudes can be found. Furthermore, an analogous problem threatens the ideal observer theory. For what sort of disapproval is it that the ideal observer has to feel in order for something to be wrong? To say, simply, "disapproval" is inadequate. The ideal observer might, for example, feel aesthetic disapproval without there being anything morally wrong. If Oswald does a dance that an ideal observer would disapprove of on purely aesthetic grounds, Oswald has not yet done anything morally wrong. But, if we say "moral disapproval," what does that come to over and above "the judgment that something is wrong?" To define "X is wrong" as "an ideal observer would feel moral disapproval of X" is very much like defining "X is wrong" as "an ideal observer would think that X is wrong." And that would be circular; we would be using the term "wrong" in order to analyze the term "wrong."

Proponents of both emotivism and the ideal observer theory therefore need to specify a noncircular way to distinguish moral attitudes from nonmoral attitudes if they are to escape triviality or circularity. On the other hand, given such a specification, either view may be defensible and not easily distinguished from the other.

Emotivism will be hard to distinguish from the ideal observer theory because a moral attitude involves a claim, a claim the ideal observer theory seeks to explicate. You cannot sincerely adopt the attitude without accepting the claim. Not only moral attitudes involve claims in this way, as we have seen. You cannot be *happy* that Rudolsky was deported if you believe that your happiness is inappropriate or mistaken, given the facts. For that matter, you cannot *believe* that Rudolsky was deported if you believe that this belief is not warranted by the evidence. Many attitudes involve the claim that they are justified from one or another point of view. Moral attitudes involve the claim that they are justified from the moral point of view—that is, from an impartial point of view.

5. Moral principles and the ideal observer

A final point. The ideal observer theory was introduced by analogy with a theory of color properties. But there is an important disanalogy. The normal or standard perceiver.referred to in the account of colors is meant to be an idealization of an ordinary

perceiver. But the ideal observer in the ideal observer theory of
moral properties is not an idealization of an ordinary moral
judge. For the ordinary person makes an essential appeal to
moral principles in his moral reasoning, whereas there is no more
reason for the ideal observer to appeal to moral principles than
there would be for a color perceiver to appeal to the theory of
the spectrum in order to perceive color or for a music lover to
deduce his appreciation of a first movement from the principles
of harmony. The ideal observer gets everything in mind and
then reacts. This is very different from our ordinary picture of
how one reaches a moral conclusion. In morality, principles are
relevant in a way in which they are not relevant in color perception or music appreciation. Moral judgment is, so we ordinarily
suppose, a matter of principle.

Now Hume says, you will recall, that moral principles, so-
called, are really generalizations about social utility. If Hume is
right, the ideal observer will after all make use of moral principles, since we are supposing that he appeals to the facts. But
we must consider more carefully whether Hume's answer covers
all appeals to principle in morality.

Hume's answer certainly works for some cases. Some moral
principles simply represent general beliefs about the facts. For
example, political principles associated with conservatism and
liberalism often represent different views of economics. Consider the principle that in times of shortage it is wrong for a large
corporation to take advantage of the situation by raising prices
so as to make huge profits. Whether or not you accept this
principle depends largely on your economic beliefs about the
long term effects of a relatively free market versus a relatively
managed economy.

But there are other issues of principle that do not fit into this
pattern. Consider arguments over abortion or over whether
people ought to become vegetarians. Such arguments involve
appeal to general principle in a different way. Appeal to principle is an essential part of such arguments. Anyone can appreciate the force of the question, "How can you justify abortion
without justifying infanticide?" or "How can you justify eating
pigs but not babies?" "What principle distinguishes these cases?"
we are asked; and it seems to be a legitimate question. We feel
compelled to answer such a question if we want to continue to

believe that there is a moral difference between the cases.

There is something about morality that leads us to suppose that moral judgments have to be defended by an appeal to principle that distinguishes apparently similar cases for which different verdicts are reached. This is an important difference between morality and aesthetics, since you may think that one melody is good, another banal, without feeling compelled to find aesthetic principles that would distinguish them.

This is related to a point mentioned earlier. Emotivism and the ideal observer theory are not specifically moral theories. They could just as easily be put forward as theories of aesthetic properties. In fact, they seem more suited to aesthetics than to morality, because aesthetic judgment is more a matter of appreciation than of decision based on principle.

Nevertheless, this does not mean that the ideal observer theory has been shown not to apply to morality. The ideal observer theories can point out, quite correctly, that it is not obviously relevant whether the ideal observer uses moral principles. The ideal observer is not intended to be an idealization of someone reaching a moral decision. The relation between our judgments and the ideal observer's reactions is different. What is needed is that the ideal observer theory account for our appeals to principle. There is no theoretical reason why the ideal observer need appeal to principle.

When we ask what principle distinguishes abortion from infanticide, we are—according to the ideal observer theory— asking not about the principles of an ideal observer but about the reactions of an ideal observer. We are asking for some reason to think that an ideal observer would react differently in the two cases.

Someone who judges that abortion is morally all right but that infanticide is not, may make this judgment because he is not disinterested, not unbiased. There may be a tendency to count the needs of the infant, who seems more like us, but to discount the needs of the fetus. Similarly, racists' moral judgments will reflect a bias toward their own race; and speciecists are biased toward their own species. A speciecist bias may account for our tendency to think that it is morally all right to eat pigs but not babies.

Now an ideal observer is supposed to be disinterested. He will not be biased in favor of one race, in favor of one sex, in favor of one species, or in favor of infants over fetuses. According to the ideal observer theory, when we ask for the principle that justifies abortion but not infanticide, we are asking what there is about abortion and infanticide that would lead a disinterested observer to approve of one but not the other. Therefore, in the ideal observer theory we may be able to account for the fact that moral reasoning makes essential appeal to moral principle, even though in giving this account we must abandon at least part of our original analogy between the ideal observer theory of moral properties and a natural account of color properties.

6. A moral

Emotivism is not completely trivial; it does make one good point. To think that something is a good thing, the right thing to do, what ought to be done, and so on, are ways of being in favor of something, and to think that something is a bad thing, the wrong thing to do, what ought not to be done, and so on, are ways of being against something. This is not just a matter of stipulation; it reflects something important about moral beliefs and moral judgments. We could not plausibly *stipulate* that to think that something is a good thing is a way of being *against* something.

The ideal observer theory is not completely trivial either. It brings out the point that moral beliefs involve a claim of impartiality. This is sometimes put by saying that moral judgments are "universalizable"—if you believe that X is wrong, you must also believe that anything relevantly like X would also be wrong, no matter what people were involved, no matter how they were involved. (For example, if you think that a given situation involving you and someone else is wrong, you are committed to supposing that the same situation would be wrong if your positions were reversed.)

Combining the two points, we see that you can have moral beliefs only to the extent that you are susceptible to a kind of unbiased motivation. For, if you are in favor of something, you are to that extent motivated to try to bring it about, and to be morally in favor of something is to favor it in an unbiased way. In the next chapter, we will begin to consider what the source of such unbiased motivation might be.

A note on further reading

The ideal observer theory is defended by Roderick Firth in "Ethical Absolutism and the Ideal Observer," *Philosophy and Phenomenological Research*, Vol. 12 (1952).

Richard B. Brandt discusses the theory in relation to other views in *Ethical Theory* (Englewood Cliffs, N.J.: Prentice-Hall, 1959), Chapters 7–11.

Jean Piaget describes stages of moral development in his book, *The Moral Judgment of the Child* translated by Marjorie Gabain (London: Kegan Paul, 1932).

III
The moral law

5 Society and superego

1. Moral rules

Morality as we ordinarily conceive it involves a number of prohibitions and requirements. You must not lie; you must not steal; you must not break your promises; you must not kill; you are to help those in need; you are to be respectful of others; you are to be grateful to those who have helped you, especially your parents; you are to be loyal to your friends; you are not to betray confidences; and so forth.

These rules make up a kind of moral law, so that moral reasoning is often much like legal reasoning. For example, killing is prohibited. Killing of people, anyway. But not all killing of people is wrong. You do not violate the moral law if you kill in self-defense. And, sometimes, you do not violate the moral law if you kill one person in order to save several others. Here is an example that philosophers have discussed.

You are driving a trolley and the brakes fail. Ahead five people are working on the track with their backs turned. Fortunately you can switch to a side track, if you act at once. Unfortunately there is also someone on that track with his back turned. If you switch your trolley to the side track, you will kill one person. If you do not switch your trolley, you will kill five people.

In such a case it would seem that the moral law would allow you to switch the trolley to the side track and kill the one person rather than kill the five people.

Compare this case with the one previously discussed in which a doctor cuts up and thereby kills a healthy patient in order to save five other patients. That did seem morally wrong, whereas running into the worker on the side track does not seem wrong—at least it does not seem obviously wrong in the way that the doctor's action seemed obviously wrong.

In considering these and similar cases, we find ourselves searching for differences that would account for our intuitive judgments. In doing this, we reason like lawyers, or like judges. For example, in attempting to account for the difference in these two cases, we may come to accept what has been called the principle of "Double Effect." According to this principle, there is an important distinction between what you aim at, either as one of your ends or as a means to one of your ends, and what you merely foresee happening as a consequence of your action. It is much worse, for example, to aim at injury to someone, either as an end or a means, than to aim at something that you know will lead to someone's injury. Doing something that will cause injury to someone is bad enough; but, according to the principle of Double Effect, it is even worse to aim at such injury. Now, the driver of the trolley does not aim at injury to the worker on the side track. If the worker leaps aside and is saved, that does not interfere with the trolley driver's goal. If the worker is injured, that is a *side effect* of what the trolley driver does; it is not part of his *means* of saving the other workers. But the doctor does aim at injury to the healthy patient he cuts up for the sake of his other five patients. If the healthy patient were to escape, that would disrupt the doctor's plan. The cutting up of this patient is the doctor's means of saving the other patients; it is not just a side effect of what the doctor does. Therefore, according to the principle of Double Effect, it is much worse to save the other patients than for the trolley driver to run into the worker on the side track, even though in both cases five lives are saved and one is lost.

The evidence that our morality incorporates principles like the principle of Double Effect is just that some such principles are needed in order to account for our intuitive moral judgments. Of course, whether or not our morality actually involves this principle, rather than another, cannot be established by this brief discussion. But this discussion should be adequate to indicate that our moral system is a complex one. Moral reasoning often involves fine distinctions of a sort that have the characteristic of law. So, if morality is not a delusion, there must be a moral law, or something like it.

This idea, that there is something like a moral law, is reflected in our use of language. We speak of moral obligations, moral duties, moral rights, and moral excuses; and these notions—duty, right, obligation, and excuse—would seem to make sense only relative to some sort of law. For instance, they have no application in judgments of aesthetics or prudence; there are no aesthetic or prudential obligations, duties, or rights. (It is true that we sometimes say that someone "owes it to himself" to do a given thing, but this is a metaphorical way of speaking.)

The point carries over to words like "ought," "must," and "may." Although these words have nonmoral uses, each is also used in a particularly moral sense and, in this sense, to say, for example, that you ought to do something is to say that it is your moral obligation or duty to do it. Since judgments about obligation and duty make sense only relative to some sort of law, these moral "ought" judgments also make sense only relative to some sort of law.

The point may be blurred by the systematic ambiguity of these words. Each of these words has at least a fourfold ambiguity. There is for example an "ought" of expectation, as when we say that the train ought to be here by now. There is also an "ought" of evaluation, as when we say that there ought to be more love in the world, meaning that it would be better if there were more love in the world, without implying that someone in particular is under any obligation to see to it that there is more love in the world. Then there is an "ought" of reasons, as when we say that a thief ought to wear gloves, meaning that he has a reason to do so. Finally, there is the moral "ought," as when we say that the thief ought not to steal. This "ought" is like the "ought" of reasons except that it is used more restrictively to indicate moral reasons. These reasons, I have suggested, must derive from something like a moral law. (More will be said about the senses of "ought" in Chapter 7.)

2. The moral sanction

Now, it is the mark of law that it has sanctions. Who then enforces the moral law? Is it society? Is social pressure the sanction? The difficulty with this otherwise plausible idea is that society can enforce only principles that are generally accepted by members of society; and we all agree that what morality dictates and what society dictates are not always the same. So, the moral law cannot be simply the law society enforces by social pressure.

But something like that idea may be right. For consider how morality is learned. At first, "X is wrong" or "X is bad" means something like "Mommy and Daddy do not want me to do X." The child's concept of his parents is of omniscient omnipotent beings whose love is all important to him; he tries to please them so that they will love him and not punish him. But he is not always sure what they want. He needs a way to predict their desires. So he uses his imagination. He tries to imagine how his parents would react to various things he might do. He tries to put himself in their place to see how he would react if he were they. He comes in this way to pretend in his imagination that he is a parent and then he tries to act so as to please this imagined pretend parent. To use the Freudian terminology, the child develops a "superego" or an "ego-ideal." He internalizes certain moral requirements. These are not necessarily the same requirements his parents placed upon him, since the superego is a modified and idealized parent and may be either stricter or more lenient than the child's actual parents, for reasons psychoanalysts find interesting.

But we do not need to assume anything about psychoanalytic theory. Whatever the psychoanalytic details, the psychological mechanism in question is not especially obscure. It can be observed, for example, when an athlete internalizes an imaginary coach. The athlete speaks to himself as a coach would, encouraging himself to play harder and better, chastising himself for errors and mistakes. He pretends to be his own coach. He does this in order to get himself to play better and more accurately and, often, he is harder on himself than an actual coach would be.

In the same way, the child comes to internalize principles of morality. Having formed a superego, the child then tries to retain its love and avoid its punishment. Thus, "X is wrong" comes to mean something like "X is incompatible with the demands of my superego." Of course, the child himself is his superego. He is his own superego to the extent that he adopts the role of his own parents. In trying to act morally, then, the child is trying to obtain his own love and respect. This continues after the child has grown up and become an adult. Inasmuch as the adult tries to act morally, he tries to act so as to retain the love and respect of that part of himself that plays the role of his imaginary parents.

Morality therefore has a social force. In the first instance, society acting through parents, enforces a social moral law. Children internalize this law by forming a superego in the idealized image of their parents. And this suggests that the complex details of this moral law are to be explained historically, perhaps in terms of social function. Society functions better if people generally tell the truth, keep their promises, do not steal, do not kill each other, and so forth. The requirements of the moral law therefore need not be in any narrow sense requirements of reason alone. There need be nothing *a priori* about morality, from the point of view of any individual, although certain moral requirements may be needed if society is to survive at all and these requirements would, in a sense, be necessary to morality.

This is not to say that the moral law is exactly the same as the law society enforces. We earlier criticized that idea as inconsistent with the plain fact that what is right can clearly conflict with what most members of society believe to be right and therefore enforce. We are now in a position to see that, nevertheless, something like that idea may be correct. The individual's morality can derive from a law society enforces without being the same as that law in every respect. Your superego is an idealized version of your parents, who in the first instance are the people who transmit society's demands to you. Your parents' demands may not coincide exactly with the demands other parents make of their children and, furthermore, your idealized version of your parents may differ from the actual version in any number of ways.

Now, a person may or may not go on to identify his imaginary parent with God. If he does, his morality will take the form of a divine law morality. This may seem to have the disadvantage that, if there is no God, his morality will rest on a fiction. But the nonreligious adult seems to be in an even worse position. His morality rests on a fiction whether or not God exists, since his morality rests on the pretend commands of an imagined parent.

3. Can morality be assessed?

It is probably true that the psychological mechanisms that lead to the development of the superego are socially useful. For morality is socially useful and the development of the superego is what makes people act morally (when they do). The superego is therefore a socially useful fiction. But it is a fiction—a pretense. That is the point. Morality rests on pretense and fiction. And it is no defense of morality and of the fiction on which it rests to say that morality is socially useful. Given the moral point of view, we have a reason to retain anything that is socially useful. But it is circular reasoning to defend the superego in this way. That is to say no more than that we have a moral reason to preserve morality. Since this moral reason rests on a fiction, it is only a fictional reason.

But the habit you develop of pretending to be an idealized parent is, for various reasons, not an easy habit to modify or get rid of, resting as it does on your earliest longings for the love of your parents. There is no easy way to abandon your superego and therefore no easy way to abandon morality. It is not enough, for example, simply to decide after psychological and philosophical reflection that morality is a gigantic pretense. The superego will not disappear quietly. It represents a habit of acting that is embedded in your personality structure, which serves deep psychological needs by allowing you to identify with your parents, a habit defended by psychological mechanisms of repression that make it very hard to come to grips with.

Nevertheless, it would seem that you ought at least to be able to raise the question whether it is rational to be moral—in other words, whether it is rational to allow yourself to follow the dictates of your superego. Of course, given the strength of the superego, it may be rational to follow its dictates in the sense that otherwise it will punish you with intense feelings of guilt and make you unhappy. Still, it would seem that you also ought to be able to ask whether it would or would not be better if you could abandon the superego, for example, through intensive psycho-analysis.

But it is not so clear that such a question makes sense. Your standards of judgment derive from your superego, so, unless there is an internal conflict among those standards, it would seem that you must agree that forming and retaining the superego is desirable.

What makes you feel uneasy about this is the suspicion that in a different society you would have internalized different moral standards. In that case, when you got around to asking whether it was rational to act in accordance with *those* standards, you would have to make your judgment on the basis of those very standards, and again, unless there was an internal conflict in the standards themselves, it would seem that you would have to agree that internalizing and retaining *those* standards was desirable.

Now, someone else who has in this way internalized moral standards that differ from those you have internalized cannot be said to act irrationally when he acts in accordance with his standards, even if his action is wrong according to your standards. For he will judge, on the basis of his standards, that it is you who act wrongly, not him, and who is to say which of you is right? Therefore, it seems possible that, when you form your superego, you internalize principles that are not determined by rationality alone, since someone else, equally rational, in another society, might internalize principles that differ from yours.

This suggests one way in which you might hope to reach an independent judgment of sorts about the moral principles you have internalized. You might hope to discover the extent to which these principles contain universal principles that should be accepted by any rational being and the extent to which your morality contains principles that go beyond what is required by rationality alone.

It might emerge that when you learn morality you learn two things. First, you learn the customs of your society. Second, you learn certain universal principles of rationality, among them the principle that, other things being equal, you should adhere to the customs of the local group. In that case, differences in custom from one group to another would not be a sign of differences in basic moral principle. There would instead be a universal morality consisting of principles of practical rationality. In an important sense, moral relativism would be false.

We will discuss in the next chapter this idea that morality can be identified with practical rationality.

On the other hand, it may be that the constraints of practical rationality are insufficient to yield a universal morality. In that case, a number of things might be true. One possibility is that learning morality consists in developing personal moral principles you accept as your own principles, no matter what others accept as their principles. In that case, even though the principles you accept have a social source, because of your upbringing, that is a fact about their origin rather than their content. Your principles would be your own in the sense in which your likes and dislikes are your own, even though to some extent they reflect your social environment and upbringing. We will discuss in Chapter 7 this idea that moral principles are personal principles.

Another possibility is that you come to accept basic moral principles as principles that are accepted in a group and that different groups might accept different principles. This would represent a social form of moral relativism. The social source of morality would then be reflected in the very content of moral principles. We will discuss in Chapters 8 and 9 this idea that moral principles are accepted as principles that are accepted by members of a particular group.

A note on further reading

Obligation is discussed in H. L. A. Hart, "Legal and Moral Obligation," in A. I. Melden, *Essays in Moral Philosophy* (Seattle, Wash.: University of Washington Press, 1958).

Philippa Foot discusses the principle of Double Effect in "Abortion and the Doctrine of Double Effect," in James Rachels (ed.), *Moral Problems* (New York: Harper & Row, 1971).

The way the moral "ought" presupposes a law is described in G. E. M. Anscombe, "Modern Moral Philosophy," *Philosophy*, Vol. 33 (1958).

Sigmund Freud's views on morality and the superego are presented in *Civilization and Its Discontents* (New York: Norton, 1962).

6 Laws of reason

1. The source of moral motivation

In our day-to-day moral thinking we presume that people know certain moral principles and can sometimes know what they ought to do according to those principles. We do not think that people always know what they ought morally to do, but we do think that it is sometimes possible for them to know this, and we would not morally blame someone for doing something that he could not have known was wrong. So, for example, we assume that it cannot be true that someone ought morally to have helped you in your time of need if there was no way in which he could have known that you needed help. Similarly, we normally assume that moral principles are binding only on creatures capable of knowing those principles. That is one reason why we suppose that animals and human idiots are not subject to morality; we suppose them to be incapable of knowing the relevant moral principles. If any form of moral nihilism should turn out to be correct and moral knowledge should turn out to be impossible, so that no one could ever know what he ought morally to do, it would follow, according to our usual ways of thinking, that no one could ever do anything morally wrong. Even the most moderate form of nihilism, which concedes that there are moral facts but denies that we can know them (see Chapter 3), would therefore completely undermine morality as we ordinarily think of it. Either moral knowledge is possible, or morality as we ordinarily conceive it is, in the words of the German philosopher Immanuel Kant (1724–1804) "a vain and chimerical notion."

But as we have seen in Chapters 1 and 2, if there is moral knowledge, it is a kind of knowledge that appears to not be supported by observation in at least one important respect. Moral facts (if there are any) never seem to help explain why anyone makes the particular observations he makes. This suggests that moral knowledge would have to be a kind of knowledge that can be acquired other than by observation. (This sort of knowledge is sometimes called *a priori* knowledge.) One possibility would be that basic moral principles were self-evident, like basic principles in mathematics. It is true, as we noted in Chapter 1, that mathematical principles play a role in helping explain why people observe what they observe, whereas moral principles apparently do not; but perhaps this difference, if it is real, is not crucial.

Furthermore, if there should be such *a priori knowledge* of moral principles, this knowledge would also represent a source of *a priori motivation* that does not depend on knowledge derived from observation. For, as we have learned from emotivism, to accept a moral principle is to be for or against something; and that is to be at least to some degree motivated to try to bring something about or to prevent something from happening.

Kant suggests an argument for a similar but even stronger conclusion. He says that, according to our usual conception of morality, basic moral principles are binding on all rational beings, so that, if there are any angels or intelligent Martians, they too ought to keep their promises, ought not to lie, ought not to cause unnecessary suffering, and so forth. But, as we have already noted, it is also part of our usual conception of morality that moral principles are binding only on those who can know those principles. So, if Kant's suggestion is correct, it follows from our usual conception of morality that basic moral principles can be known by all rational beings. Since to accept a moral principle is to be motivated at least to some extent to act in accordance with that principle, this means that our usual conception of morality must presuppose an *a priori* source of moral motivation in reason and rationality itself. It must be possible for any rational being to be motivated to act morally simply by thinking and reasoning without appeal to knowledge acquired through observation. Kant's conclusion is that either reason alone is such a source of motivation or morality, as we ordinarily understand it, is a vain and chimerical notion.

Now in the Humean or Aristotelian understanding of practical reasoning we mentioned earlier (in Chapter 3), practical reasoning is always means–ends reasoning. You begin with one or more ends and, through reasoning, determine the best means to obtain those ends. This leads you to adopt those means as new intermediate ends. You repeat this process and, eventually, in this way you come to adopt as such a means or an intermediate end something that is immediately within your power, which you then do. In this view, practical reasoning serves to help you satisfy your already existing desires. Desire can be an ultimate source of motivation, but practical reasoning cannot, since the function of such reasoning is simply to organize and channel already existing motivation. In this view, then, there is only one kind of practical irrationality, namely failing to arrive at means that would best satisfy your ends. There can be no irrationality in your ultimate ends themselves. Any desires at all are possible, at least in theory. None are irrational. Hume says, for example, that it is not contrary to reason to prefer the destruction of the world to the scratching of your finger. That would be irrational only if you cared more about the world than about your finger, and you may not care so much about the world.

As we have seen, Kant argues that either reason is a source of motivation, or morality is a delusion. According to the conception of practical reasoning in Hume and Aristotle, reason cannot be a source of motivation. So, *either* morality is a delusion *or* the conception of practical reasoning in Hume and Aristotle is inadequate *or* there is something wrong with Kant's argument. Reviewing that argument, we see that it assumes that three things are essential to morality as we ordinarily conceive it:

1. that a moral principle is binding only on someone who could know that principle;
2. that basic moral principles are binding on all rational beings; and
3. that to accept a moral principle is to be at least to some degree motivated so as to act in accordance with it.

Now, perhaps the weakest premise here is 2. As we shall see, below, it is not obviously *essential* to our ordinary conception of morality that moral principles be binding on all rational beings. So, if we wished to keep the Hume–Aristotle conception of practical reasoning as means–ends reasoning, we could disarm Kant's arguments by rejecting 2.

There would still be an argument for the weaker conclusion that morality presupposes *a priori* knowledge of moral principles together with some sort of *a priori* motivation. This argument assumes that 1 and 3 are essential to morality as we ordinarily conceive it:

      1. that a moral principle is binding only on someone who could know that principle; and

      3. that to accept a moral principle is to be at least to some degree motivated so as to act in accordance with it.

The argument also assumes:

      4. that, if there is any moral knowledge, there is some that lacks observational support.

Given these assumptions, it follows that morality presupposes *a priori* knowledge of moral principles and *a priori* motivation to act in accordance with those principles. But this argument does not conflict with the Hume–Aristotle conception of practical reasoning, because moral motivation could have an *a priori* source without having a source in reason alone. For example, relevant knowledge and motivation could be built into people as the result of evolution, so that people would have an innate knowledge of basic moral principles, a knowledge that was necessarily tied to certain innate goals or desires. Hume's idea that people are born with an innate tendency toward sympathy with others might be sufficient for this. And there are other possibilities as well, as we shall see.

2. Why care about someone else?

So, neither Kant's argument, nor this one, *forces* us to choose between morality and the Hume–Aristotle conception of practical reasoning. Neither argument *proves* that moral motivation must have its source in reason itself if morality is not to be a delusion. On the other hand, for all that we have said so far, it may be irrational not to care about other people, and not just for self-interested reasons, either. Whether or not it *pays* in the long run to develop a genuine concern for other people, it is possible that you have a reason to care about other people that does not arise from considerations of self-interest. It may be as irrational not to care about other people as it is not to care about yourself. Perhaps reasons for caring can be found in the very nature of reason and rationality. This, in any event, is the Kantian suggestion, which we must now examine.

Let us consider a specific case, Austin P. Jones, a totally self-interested individual, who is taking a leisurely drive along a seldom used and isolated road. Ahead he sees a stopped car, and the driver, who is apparently out of gas, is trying to wave him down. Our question is whether Jones has any reason to help the stranded motorist. Would it be irrational for him to ignore that motorist and continue on his way?

Now, it may or may not be true that Jones should have tried to develop a concern for others earlier in his life. Perhaps his life would now be happier if he had done so. And, in that sense, perhaps it is irrational for him not to care now about the stranded motorist. But that is not the point. We are to suppose that it is now too late for Jones to change his stripes. He is fixed in his ways, and as he is now, he has no concern for others. He does not particularly dislike them; he just does not care one way or another about them. So, in the present instance, he observes the plight of the stranded motorist with detached amusement and without feeling the slightest motivation to help. The question we must answer is whether, given Jones's present lack of concern for others, he nevertheless has a reason to stop and help. Do the needs of the stranded motorist give him any such reason, even though he does not care about the stranded motorist? Is it irrational for him to drive past without stopping?

We might try out the following argument on Jones. "If the situation were reversed, you would need help and your needs would give him a reason to help you. So—by parity of reasoning—his needs must now provide you with a reason to help him." That might be a good argument, if we could get Jones to agree that his own need for help would provide a reason for another person to help him. But Jones might not agree. He might maintain, for example, that only self-interest can give a person a reason to do something.

On the other hand, we sometimes do convince a self-interested person to do something by an argument in which we ask him to consider what it would be like if the situation were reversed. This can happen even when he knows very well that the situation will never be reversed, at least as regards the person who needs help on this occasion. So, when we use such an argument to convince a self-interested person, we need not be convincing him that it is in his self-interest to help on this occasion. Instead we convince him that he has a reason to help, a reason not based on self-interest. It is striking that, by reasoning in this way, we can get a self-interested person to act for such a reason.

This suggests two conclusions. It suggests, first, that the fact that you would want the other person to help you, if the situation were reversed, really may be itself a reason for you to help him in this situation—quite apart from considerations of self-interest. If so, Jones has a reason to stop to help the stranded motorist, whether he realizes it or not, and he acts irrationally if he drives past without stopping. Second, this suggests that reasoning can get you to act, not just by revealing how your action is a means to what you already desire but also by showing you that you have a reason to act whether or not you want to.

3. Desires as data

In other words, this suggests a theory of reasoning like Kant's, or like the one elegantly defended by the contemporary American philosopher, Thomas Nagel, in *The Possibility of Altruism.* * In such a theory, reason is the motivating source. In deciding what to do, you ask yourself what you have reasons to do. Some of these reasons may derive from your present desires, but others may not. You then try to do whatever you have the best reasons to do.

Nagel gives as an example the fact that you may buy yourself groceries even though you are not hungry when you do so. You buy the groceries because you know that you are going to be hungry later. You suppose that your future desire for food gives you a reason to shop now. According to the Hume–Aristotle conception, this should be impossible. A future desire cannot in that view give you a reason now to do something. But in Nagel's

*Oxford, Oxford University Press, 1970.

Kantian conception of practical reasoning, you can have a reason to do something that does not derive from any antecedent desire you currently have. Indeed, according to Nagel, it is a principle of practical rationality that, if you are going to have a certain desire, you now have a reason to do something that will facilitate the satisfaction of that desire, whether or not you have a present desire.

Hume or Aristotle would have to say that you will be motivated to buy groceries only if you have some sort of prior desire—such as the desire that your future desires should be satisfied. But, as Nagel observes, this threatens the Hume–Aristotle conception with circularity. For what criterion is to be used to determine whether there is such a prior desire? If the test is simply whether there is any motivation, then it is trivially true that where there is motivation there is prior desire; but that is no objection to Nagel's Kantian theory. Nagel observes that this desire to satisfy your future desires, if it is even proper to say that there is such a desire, is not a desire of the same sort as a desire for food or water. He argues that its source lies not in some transitory state of the body but rather in the nature of personal identity and reason itself. It is, according to Nagel, a desire that it would be irrational not to have; you are irrational if you do not care about the future, if you know that in the future you are going to care.

The Hume–Aristotle conception of practical reasoning and Nagel's Kantian conception treat basic desires differently. For Hume and Aristotle, such basic desires as hunger and thirst are forces or energy that reason directs and organizes. In their conception, reason itself provides no energy and no force. In Nagel's more Kantian theory, basic desires are not forces or energy but a kind of data. When you reason, your information includes the fact that you have or will have certain desires. These desires influence what you will do because you take them to give you reasons to do things and you tend to do what you think you have reasons to do. But present desires give you no more reason to do something than future desires do and it is irrational to satisfy only present desires at the expense of future desires.

Now, according to Nagel, just as your own future desires can give you a present reason to do something, so can the desires of other people. In Nagel's view, you have a reason to do whatever will promote the satisfaction of any desire—your own or another

person's, it does not matter. If you can help another person and
do not have any reason not to, then it is as irrational for you not to
help that person as it is for you to fail to provide for the satisfaction of your own future desires. Therefore, in Nagel's view,
Jones has a reason to stop to help the stranded motorist and it
would be irrational for Jones to drive on by without helping.
Hume and Aristotle would not agree; they would say that the
desires of other people can give you reasons to do things only if
you have a prior desire, for example, that other people's desires
should be satisfied. But Nagel holds that this sort of prior desire
is not a basic bodily desire, like hunger or thirst, and is rather
itself a reflection of the way in which practical reasoning works;
so, according to Nagel, it is irrational not to have that desire. If
Nagel is right, a concern for others is built into the very structure
of practical reasoning—and, inasmuch as moral motivation reflects such a concern for others, the source of such motivation is
to be found in reason itself.

But two points must be made about Nagel's theory. First, he
has not proven that it is irrational not to care about other people
or even irrational not to care what will happen to you in the
future. Second, Nagel's conception of the source of moral motivation as deriving from a rational concern for the interests of
other people does not in itself explain why there should be
anything like a moral law. For example, it does not explain why
we should distinguish, as we do, between the doctor who cuts up
a healthy patient to save five other patients and the doctor who
saves five patients rather than one patient (Chapter 1) or the
trolley driver who kills the one worker on the side track rather
than the five workers on the main track (Chapter 5). Inasmuch as
the interests of the other people provide an agent with reasons to
promote those interests, it is hard to see on what basis these cases
might be distinguised.

4. Kant's test

Kant is particularly concerned to bring out the way in which
morality involves a moral law, although he never (as far as I
know) addresses himself to the particular question just raised.
Kant's basic idea is that acting morally is acting out of respect for
principles that any rational being would accept. These principles, according to Kant, make up the moral law. It is not enough

simply to act in accordance with those principles; it is not enough to "do the right thing." A storeowner who regularly gives the right change even to children because it is good for business to do so is not necessarily acting morally, even though he is acting as if he were. Whether or not an act is moral depends on why you do it. You must do it because it is the right thing to do. If you do it only for other reasons, your act has no moral worth, according to Kant. He says that an act has moral worth only if you do it because it is right, because it is required by the moral law—that is to say, because it is required by a law that all rational beings would accept.

Kant assumes that, whenever you act for a reason, your action always depends on a basic or an ultimate principle. (He often calls this principle your "maxim.") For example, if you act so as to satisfy your desires, your basic principle or maxim is to act so as to satisfy your desires. Now, according to Kant, if you are to act morally, your basic principle or maxim must be a principle that you accept as a principle for all rational beings. In Kant's terminology, you must "will" your principle as a universal law for all rational beings. Therefore, he supposes that one test of the principle on which you act is whether you agree to everyone's acting on that principle and, in order to determine whether you could agree to that, you should always act as you would act if the "maxim" or ultimate principle on which you act was going by miracle to become a universal law that everyone always acted on.

To act in that way, according to Kant, is to act from the moral law. You are therefore also acting as if everyone was by miracle going to act from the moral law. You are therefore acting as you would in a world in which everyone acted from the moral law at all times. In such a world, each person would have unconditional moral worth, according to Kant, for he argues that the only thing that has unconditional moral worth is someone trying to do what is right. Something of unconditional moral worth is an "end" in Kant's terminology. That is one reason why Kant says that in acting morally you act as if you were legislating for a Kingdom of Ends. What this amounts to is something like the Golden Rule, "Do unto others as you would have them do unto you," except that Kant's rule concerns only ultimate principles of action—the ultimate principles from which you act should be principles that you would choose to have as the ultimate principles on which everyone acted.

As Kant understands this test, it involves a kind of regress or circle, because the principle you would choose to have everyone act on is also the principle behind that very choice. In other words, in Kant's view, you act rationally and therefore morally in doing D only if there is a principle P such that

1. you do D;
2. your ultimate principle in doing what you do in 1 is P;
3. you would choose P as an ultimate principle on which everyone would act; and
4. your ultimate principle in doing what you do in 3 is P.

If you choose to have certain principles adopted by everyone because you suppose that it would be in your self-interest to have those principles adopted, then your ultimate principle is really pure self-interest, so the issue is whether you would out of self-interest choose that everyone should act ultimately out of pure self-interest. Presumably you would not choose that, since it is not in your self-interest that everyone always act out of pure self-interest. On the other hand, you might choose a principle like the Golden Rule as an ultimate principle, because that could provide you with a reason to choose that everyone act on that principle. If you choose the Golden Rule, your reason for choosing it would have to be that choosing the Golden Rule for everyone to follow is doing unto others what you would have them do unto you. Your ultimate reasons for choosing to have certain reasons as everyone's ultimate reasons must, in Kant's view, be those very reasons themselves.

Your ultimate principle will have to *include* self-interest, since (Kant thinks) any rational being is necessarily self-interested. But your principle must go beyond mere self-interest, too, since it is not in your self-interest that everyone should act solely out of self-interest. Therefore, your principle must allow for enough altruism and other non-self-interested motivation so that, given these further motives in addition to self-interest, it would be rational to choose that everyone always act from such motives. Kant thinks that there is a unique outcome to this test and that the resulting principle will include, not only self-interest and a limited altruism, but also rules about property, promising, and so forth—

in fact, the usual principles of morality. But he does not prove that his test yields a unique outcome in this way.

Indeed, for reasons we need not go into here, Kant believes that you cannot ever *know* that there is a moral law—a law that derives from reason alone. He argues, however, that whenever you act you must implicitly assume that there is such a law. For whenever you are deciding what to do, you must think of your impending decision in the Kantian way rather than the Humean or Aristotelian way. You must be able to suppose that you are free to decide one way or another. You must suppose that you are going to make your decision for certain reasons. You therefore cannot suppose that your decision is simply the result of a number of forces, represented by your desires. To think of your desires in this way, simply as forces (as in the Hume–Aristotle conception), would be to think of them as compulsions not under your control. It is true that sometimes you do see your desires as compulsions; but normally you do not. Normally, you treat your desires as data in the way described by Kant and Nagel. You think of yourself as acting for a reason. If you did not, you could not suppose that you were deciding anything at all. Furthermore, you must suppose that you are acting rationally—that your ultimate reasons are good reasons.

Kant does not think that you can know whether you or anyone else ever decides in this sense to act. He thinks that it is possible that your actions are always the blind result of competing desires and that you never act for one or another reason. Nevertheless, he argues that you normally assume that there are reasons why you do what you do. Your assumption that you act for reasons is what Kant calls a "practical postulate." It is unprovable but necessary to your conception of yourself as an agent.

Now Kant argues, finally, that this implies that, when you act, you must postulate the moral law as the ultimate test of rationality. For, when you act, you must assume you are acting for a reason and must therefore assume that there is an ultimate principle or a reason behind your action. Moreover, you must also assume that it is rational for you to act from your ultimate principle or reason, which means, according to Kant, that you must assume that your ultimate reason is a reason for any rational being. (For, if your principle is to do D and you think that there is a rational being for whom it is not rational to do D, then your *ultimate* principle is not simply to do D but, rather to do D if you are a being of a certain sort.) So, you must be willing to accept not only your own acting from this ultimate reason but everyone else's acting as well. Therefore, Kant concludes, when you act, you must will your ultimate principle or reason (or "maxim") as a universal law for all rational beings; otherwise you are irrational. But, Kant observes, that is just the moral law as he understands it; so he concludes that, whenever you act, you must postulate the moral law as an ultimate test of rationality.

5. Objections to Kant

Kant's argument depends upon an ambiguity concerning what is involved in accepting a principle. Suppose that your ultimate principle is to try to maximize your own happiness. Then you must think that this principle is a rational one; in other words, you must think that it is rational for you to try to maximize your own happiness. Since this is your ultimate principle, you must also think that it would be rational for anyone else to try to maximize his own happiness. (For, if you thought that only people of type Q would be rational to try to maximize their own happiness, your ultimate principle would not be simply to try to maximize your own happiness but, rather, e.g., to try if you are a person of type Q to maximize your own happiness.) There is therefore a sense in which you must accept everyone's acting on your basic principle; for you must agree that it is rational for them to do so. But it does not follow that you must accept this in the sense that you have to *want* everyone to act on that principle; so Kant has not shown that there is any mistake in the thought that it would be rational for everyone to try to maximize their own happiness, although you do not want them to do so. Therefore Kant has not shown that there is anything irrational in acting purely from self-interest.

Kant's test of moral principles is similarly defective. For one thing, since you can agree that it would be rational for everyone to act on your basic principle without being committed to wanting them to do so, you can also agree to this without having to agree that it would be rational on the basis of your principle to bring it about that everyone acted on that principle (if by miracle you could accomplish this). Furthermore, even apart from the question whether moral principles are laws of reason, it cannot be true that the correct moral principles are limited to those principles that would apply in a Kingdom of Ends, where everyone acted morally and no one ever did anything wrong. In the real world not everyone acts morally and moral principles must allow for that. Total pacifism might be a good principle if everyone were to follow it. But not everyone is, so it isn't.

Kant unsuccessfully tries to show that the moral law, as a law of reason, can be derived from an analysis of what it is to act freely or to decide to do something. He tries to show that when you think of yourself as an agent you must postulate principles of rationality that constitute the moral law. It is true that Kant's conception of practical reasoning (especially as it is elaborated and refined by Nagel) is a more plausible conception than Hume's or Aristotle's, which treats desires as forces. This conception, however, does not yield the results Kant seeks.

This leaves us with Kant's earlier argument that either moral motivation derives from reason alone, or morality is a vain and chimerical notion. But, as noted earlier, there is a way round that argument, too. We can simply deny Kant's assumption that basic moral principles are binding on all rational beings. This suggests a more relativistic conception of morality, in which each person's moral principles are his own and rational beings do not necessarily assume that they all share the same fundamental principles. We shall examine such a conception of morality in the next chapter.

A note on further reading

The best statement of Immanuel Kant's moral theory is in his *Foundations of the Metaphysics of Morals*. There is a more readable and less rigorous version in his *Lectures on Ethics*, which is based on student notes. Also relevant are Kant's *Critique of Practical Reason* and his *Religion Beyond the Limits of Reason Alone*.

The most useful commentary on Kant's moral theory in English is Thomas Nagel's defense of a similar view in his *Possibility of Altruism* (Oxford: Oxford University Press, 1970).

7 Personal principles

1. A personal moral law

A number of philosophers have been greatly influenced by
Kant's account of morality without agreeing with his views about
the powers of reason. Although these philosophers do not believe
that the principles that must be accepted by all rational beings
are strong enough to constitute what we normally think of as
morality, they do think that Kant's analysis is largely correct in
other respects. For instance, they agree that when you act you
must think of yourself as acting from reasons and cannot think
that you are simply being pulled along by your strongest desires;
otherwise you would have to think of yourself as acting under
compulsion or even as not acting at all. They also agree that to
act from reasons is to act on principles and that these principles
can provide you with reasons only if they are rational principles.

Now Kant thought, as we have seen, that this meant that the
relevant principles had to be principles that any rational agent
would accept—therefore it would be irrational for any agent not
to accept those principles. The post-Kantian philosophers I am
talking about do not agree. They believe that the only rational
constraints on a system of principles are requirements of simple
consistency. So they hold that different people can have different principles, principles that give them reasons to do different

and conflicting things, without any of them being irrational, as long as each person's principles are internally consistent.

Let us suppose that these other philosophers are right about the powers of reason. Then, if, with Kant, we limit moral principles to those principles that are required by reason, morality must shrink to mere consistency. And, indeed, this is the view of the contemporary French existentialist J. P. Sartre, who thinks for this reason that morality amounts to what he calls "good faith"; acting morally consists solely in not being hypocritical. *
On the other hand, we can identify each person's morality with that person's whole system of principles and not just with those principles required by reason. This is roughly what the contemporary English philosopher of language R. M. Hare does, although Hare does not count any principle whatsoever as a moral principle, as we shall see.† In his view, different people can have different moralities, since they can have different principles that they accept as moral principles, without their being irrational.

Compared with our usual conception of morality, Sartre's view seems too weak and Hare's too strong. Sartre's view seems too weak because we ordinarily suppose that there is more to morality than good faith and not being hypocritical. We ordinarily suppose that morality requires that you not steal, not lie, help those in distress, and so forth. Such requirements must involve more than simply being true to yourself unless Kant is right about the powers of reason.

On the other hand, Hare's view gives content to morality but not in what we would ordinarily think the right way. In our ordinary view, morality itself imposes requirements on a person; and the fact that someone decides to adopt a certain principle as his own does not make it one of his moral principles unless he adopts it because he thinks that action in accordance with that principle is required by morality. Furthermore, the principles Hare counts as a person's moral principles need not coincide with what we would ordinarily take to be the principles of morality. There is no reason, in his view, why someone would have to adopt principles against lying and stealing and for help-

---

*"Existentialism is a Humanism," in Kaufmann (ed.) *Existentialism: From Dostoevsky to Sartre*, New York, Meridian: 1956.

†*The Language of Morals*, Oxford, The Clarendon Press: 1952.

ing others in distress. A person's moral principles, in Hare's view, may be quite different from what we would ordinarily think of as the principles of morality.

But conflicts with our ordinary conception of morality cannot refute either Hare's or Sartre's theory, because it is open to either philosopher to reply that our ordinary conception of morality presupposes a false view of reason. If the requirements of reason are much lower than we ordinarily assume, as Hare and Sartre believe, then it is possible that our ordinary conception of morality cannot be sustained. Perhaps, morality as we ordinarily conceive it is a "vain and chimerical notion"—a delusion. That would not mean that we had to do without morality in any sense at all, though. And, given a choice, whether we decided to talk in Sartre's way or in Hare's way might turn out to be a purely verbal matter.

2. R. M. Hare's theory

Hare's theory is somewhat more elaborately worked out than Sartre's, as it happens, so let us consider Hare's in more detail. He postulates that a person's basic moral principles can be expressed as general imperatives of the form, "For any person P, at any time when P is in circumstances C, let P do D!" For example, "Let any person who has promised to do something do what he has promised to do!" These principles are supposed to be general and exceptionless. They are supposed to be general in that they are addressed to everyone. They are supposed to be exceptionless in that they are to hold in any situation that might arise, without exception, including merely hypothetical situations. Therefore, any potential exceptions have to be "built into" the principles in advance. For example, if we build in potential exceptions to our principle about promise-keeping, we might end up with something like this:

> Let any person who has promised to do something, where the promise was neither obtained under false pretences nor by means of coercion, do what he has promised to do, unless he could do something else that is incompatible with keeping his promise that would be of significant service to someone who needs help, in which case let him do that other thing!

Actually, even such an elaborate principle is hopelessly over-simplified compared with the sorts of principles most people would have to accept if their morality really were based on principles of this kind. (We will return to this point in Chapter 10.)

Now, according to Hare, to accept a general principle as a moral principle is (a) to intend to adhere to it yourself and (b) to intend to try to get others to accept it. Condition (b) expresses the generality or universality of the principle. It is not just a principle for yourself. It does not just say, for example, "At any time when I am in circumstances C, let me do D!"

As Hare observes, this constrains your moral principles. They cannot be directed simply to the promotion of your own narrow self-interest, since you must be in favor of your principles being followed not only by you but by all others as well—and not only in the present situation but in the merely hypothetical situations in which the positions of you and the various others are reversed. Nevertheless, there is no uniquely rational set of principles that satisfies this constraint. Different people will accept different and conflicting sets of principles that satisfy (a) and (b).

Someone might accept only weaker principles that satisfy (a) but not (b). He would intend to follow his principles himself but would not be interested in trying to get others to follow them. For example, he might in this way accept purely egoistic principles he does not want other people to follow, because it is not in his self-interest that other people follow egoistic principles. Such a person would not be obviously irrational. Reason does not seem to require that you adopt general principles that satisfy both (a) and (b). It is true that, if you think of yourself as acting from reasons (and not just as someone who is a victim of his desires), then you must assume that the reasons you act from are good reasons. That implies that you must assume that anyone else in an identical position would have the same good reasons to act as you do. But that does not imply that you are prepared or ought to be prepared to get other people to act similarly for similar reasons. Indeed, if you are an egoist, you ought to try to keep others from acting on what you think are the most rational principles for them to act on. Rationality alone does not require you to act from principles that satisfy condition (b).

But if your principles satisfy only condition (a), and you do not intend to try to get others to adopt them, Hare will not count them "moral principles." According to Hare, to have moral principles is to have principles that you intend to follow and also intend to try to get others to follow. So rationality alone does not force you to have moral principles in Hare's sense of "moral principle."

Given this account of moral principles, Hare is prepared to give a rough definition of the moral "ought." He says that "P ought to do D" means something like "P's doing D is in accordance with the general moral principles to which I hereby subscribe," and this in turn means something like, "the facts taken together with the general moral principles to which I hereby subscribe imply the imperative addressed to P, 'Do D!'"

The phrase, "to which I hereby subscribe," is needed in order to allow for moral disagreement. For suppose that the analysis goes simply: "P ought to do D" means "P's doing D is in accordance with the general moral principles that I subscribe to." Then if I say that P ought to do D and you say that P ought not to do D, we would not even be disagreeing, according to the analysis. For I would be saying that P's doing D is in accordance with the principles to which I subscribe and you would be saying that P's not doing D is in accordance with the principles to which you subscribe. And these remarks do not contradict each other, since you and I may have different principles.

How, then, do we disagree? According to Hare, we disagree in attitude, because we are advocating conflicting principles. I am advocating principles that would require P to do D, whereas you are advocating principles that would require P not to do D. When I say that P's doing D is in accordance with principles to which I hereby subscribe, my "hereby" is a sign that I am not just describing my principles but am in that very utterance subscribing to them; in other words, I am advocating them. You and I differ in that we are advocating incompatible things.

Now we also disagree if I say that P ought to do D and you simply deny this, without going on to say that P ought not to do D. In that case, our disagreement is not just that I am advocating principles that require P to do D, whereas you are advocating principles that do not require P to do D, for that might mean only that I was advocating stronger principles than you were; and my principles can be stronger than yours without conflicting with yours. In fact, however, when you deny that P ought to do

D, you are not just advocating principles that do not require P to do D, you are also advocating that people not accept as moral principles any that taken together would require P to do D. In other words, you are advocating that people adopt, as their total set of moral principles, principles that do not require P to do D.

So, extending Hare's analysis to the denials of moral "ought" sentences, we see that "it is not the case that P ought to do D" should be analyzed as meaning something like, "I hereby subscribe to and advocate that people adopt as their total set of moral principles, principles M, which are such that it is not the case that P's doing D is in accordance with M." Similarly, when the moral "ought" appears embedded in a subordinate clause of any larger sentence, it should be analyzed like this: ". . . P ought to do D . . ." means something like "I hereby subscribe to and advocate that people adopt as their total set of moral principles, principles M such that . . . P's doing D is in accordance with M. . . ."

Hare observes that there is another use of the moral "ought," whereby the speaker does not subscribe to the relevant principles. He calls this the inverted commas use, since the principles are those advocated by someone else.* For example, "Jones believes that P ought to do D" is not to be analyzed as "I hereby subscribe to and advocate that people adopt as their total set of moral principles, principles M such that Jones believes that P's doing D is in accordance with M." Jones is said to subscribe to certain principles, not the speaker. For such a sentence, the analysis must go something like "Jones subscribes to and intends to try to get people to adopt as their total set of moral principles principles M such that he believes that P's doing D is in accordance with M."

3. The Existentialist objection to Hare

I now want to consider an objection to Hare's analysis from the point of view of someone like Sartre, who would restrict moral principles to principles of simple consistency. Sartre and Hare both agree that it can happen that, although you and P are perfectly consistent in the principles you accept, your principles imply that P should do D whereas his principles imply that he should not do D. In such a case, Hare's analysis would still allow you to say of P that he ought to do D. The objection is that this is

*Inverted commas are quotation marks.

an odd thing to say, given that P has no reason to do D, at least
none that derives from his principles. It is part of our ordinary
view that P ought to do D only in cases in which P has reasons to
do D. And, it is unclear where those reasons might come from,
except from P's principles. For how can *your* principles give P
any reason to do D if P does not share your principles? To say
that P ought to do D is to say, at least, that P has a reason to do D.
But Hare's analysis would allow you to say that P ought to do D
even though you must agree that P has no reason to do D.
Therefore, so the objection goes, Hare's analysis must be inadequate.

Of course, you might accept, as one of your moral principles,
the principle (O) that someone ought to do something only if he
as a reason to do it. In that case, if your moral principles were
consistent, they could not imply that P ought to do D, even
though he had no reason to do D. The difficulty for Hare is that
there is nothing in his analysis that requires you to accept (O) as a
moral principle, so Hare must allow for the possibility that you
do not accept (O) and therefore that your moral principles
sometimes imply that P ought to do D even though he has no
reason to do D. The objection is that this possibility should be
ruled out.

Two replies to this objection are possible. One denies the
principle (O) that P ought to do D only if P has a reason to do D.
The other says, on the contrary, that in the relevant sense P does
have a reason to do D. Let us consider each of these replies in
turn.

First, is it true that to say that P ought to do D implies that P
has a reason to do D? In order to answer this question, we must
distinguish senses of "ought." In what we previously have called
the evaluative sense of "ought" there is no such implication. But
that is no help to Hare's analysis, since his intention is to analyze
the moral sense of "ought," which is not the same as the evaluative sense; and when "ought" is understood in its moral sense, the
implication holds.

I suggested in Chapter 5 that there are at least four senses of
"ought." There is, first of all, an "ought" of expectation, as when
you say that the train ought to be here soon. Then there is an
"ought" of evaluation, as when you say that there ought to be
more love in the world, meaning that it would be a good thing if

there were more love in the world. You do not mean that you expect that there will be more love in the world. And, in saying that the train ought to be here soon, you did not necessarily mean that it would be a good thing if the train were here soon.

These two senses of "ought,-- the "ought" of expection and the evaluative "ought," are used to describe states of affairs. "Ought" can also be used to characterize an agent more particularly. We can say that an agent ought to perform a certain act. Further-more, there are at least two different senses in which we can say this. We can use the moral "ought" to say that a person morally ought to do something; for example, speaking of a robber who is about to rob a bank, we might say that he ought to give up his plan and return home. Or we can use the "ought" of rationality; speaking of the robber, we might say that he ought to go in by the rear door, meaning that it would be rational for him to do this in order to avoid the guard by the front door. Clearly, there is a difference in what "ought" means when we say that he ought to go home as against when we say that he ought to use the rear door.

Now perhaps we can agree that there is a clear difference in sense between the "ought" of expectation, the moral "ought" and the "ought" of rationality (although if Kant were right, the moral "ought" would coincide with the "ought" of rationality). What is harder to see is any difference between the evaluative "ought" and the moral "ought." But consider the remark, "Rockefeller ought to give his money to the poor." This remark is subtly ambiguous between the evaluative and moral interpretations of "ought." It might be understood to be a remark about what ought to be, namely that it ought to be the case that Rockefeller gives his money to the poor. Or the remark might be interpreted as a remark about Rockefeller as an agent, saying that there is a certain act he morally ought to perform: Rockefeller ought mor-ally to give his money to the poor. In the one case, the speaker is saying that a certain state of affairs would be a good one. In the other case, the speaker is saying that it would be wrong of Rockefeller not to follow a certain course of action. The second remark is the stronger one. You might make the weaker remark because you think it would be nice if there were not the differ-ences in wealth that now exist. You might make the stronger remark if you think that Rockefeller made his money by exploiting the poor and therefore owes it to them. If you make the stronger remark, using the moral "ought," you imply that Rockefeller is morally wrong not to return the money. If you make the weaker remark, using the evaluative "ought," you do not necessarily imply that Rockefeller is wrong, although you do imply that a certain situation is wrong.

The evaluative "ought" is used to assess a situation: Rockefeller's giving his money to the poor. The moral "ought" is used to make a judgment about the subject of the sentence, in this case, Rockefeller. Therefore, there is a way to distinguish the evaluative "ought to be" from the moral "ought to do." If the evaluative meaning is the right one, the sentence, "Rockefeller ought to give his money to the poor," is equivalent to "It ought to be the case that Rockefeller gives his money to the poor." If the moral sense is relevant, this equivalence does not hold. Since Rockefeller giving his money to the poor is the same as the poor getting Rockefeller's money from him, if the evaluative meaning is what is intended, the sentence, "Rockefeller ought to give his money to the poor," is equivalent to the sentence, "The poor ought to get Rockefeller's money from him." If the moral sense is intended, though, these sentences cannot be equivalent, since the first then says what Rockefeller ought to do whereas the second says what the poor ought to do (if they can).

Now, Hare is attempting to analyze "P ought to do D," in which "ought" is used in its moral sense, as opposed to its probabilistic, evaluative, or rational senses. But, in the moral sense of "ought," to say that P ought to do D is to imply that P has reasons to do D, for it is inconsistent to suppose that P ought (morally) to do D when he has no reason at all—not even a moral reason—to do D.

The point will be obscured if the moral "ought" is not clearly distinguished from the evaluative "ought." In saying that Rockefeller ought to give his money to the poor, you might not be saying even in part that Rockefeller has a reason to give his money to the poor. You could say this and consistently agree that Rockefeller has no reason to give his money to the poor, if you are using the evaluative "ought." If you are saying only that it ought to be the case that Rockefeller gives his money to the poor, you are not necessarily saying that there is any moral obligation on Rockefeller to give his money to the poor and you are not necessarily implying that there are any reasons for him to do so. It is not inconsistent to suppose that, even though Rockefeller has no reason—not even a moral reason—to give his money to the poor, still it ought to be the case that he give his money to the poor; the world would be a better place. But, if you mean that Rockefeller ought morally to give his money to the poor, because for example he got the money through exploiting them, you do imply that Rockefeller has a reason to give his money to the poor, namely that he made his money by exploiting the poor. The evaluative "ought," which is an "ought to be," carries no implications about an agent's having reasons to act. The moral "ought," which is an "ought to do," does carry the implication that the person who ought to do something has a reason to do it.

4. Reasons and basic principles

We have found that the first way of replying on Hare's behalf to the Sartrean objection does not work. But we see that the second way of replying might work. The objection, you will recall, is that Hare cannot account for moral judgments you might make about a person whose principles differ from yours. To say that such a person ought to do something is to say that he has a reason to do it. But Hare would allow you to say that a person ought to do something even though the person in question does not have a reason to do it and even when he has every reason not to do it. The first reply to this Sartrean objection attempted to deny the principle (O) that to say that someone ought morally to do something is to say that he has a reason to do it. I have argued that this reply seems plausible only if you fail to distinguish the moral "ought to do" from the evaluative "ought to be." The second reply takes a different view and argues that the person in question does have a reason to do the thing in question, namely the reason that he ought to do it.

Recall the situation: P's principles differ from yours. By his principles, he ought not to do D. By your principles he ought ot do D. More exactly, P's doing D is in accord with your principles but not with his. So you say that P morally ought to do D, as Hare's analysis allows you to do. The objection was that this implies that P has a reason to do D, which he does not have. The reply that we are now considering is that when you say that P ought to do D you do think that he has a reason to do D, because

its being the case that he ought to do D is a reason for him to do
D, whether he realizes it or not. It is true that P will not himself
assume he has a reason to do D, particularly this reason. But to
say that P has a reason to do D is not to say that P himself realizes
that he has a reason to do D.

In order to make this concrete, let us suppose that one of your
principles is not to eat any meat. This is a principle you intend to
adhere to and you also intend to try to get others to accept it. So,
according to Hare, this is one of your moral principles. Now it
turns out that P has a different principle. He is in favor of eating
meat at every meal. From your principles, together with the fact
that the steak on P's plate is meat, you conclude that P ought not
to eat the steak. Furthermore, you say that P has a reason to not
eat the steak, namely that the steak is meat and one ought not to
eat any meat. You agree, however, that P does not himself
accept this principle and, indeed, accepts the opposite principle.
Is this coherent?

Of course, if P had accepted your general principle, the fact
that steak is meat would give him a reason not to eat it. But, since
he does not accept your principle, how can you suppose that this
fact does after all give him such a reason? Surely, you can
suppose that this gives him a reason only if you think that P
ought to accept your principle rather than his own. So you must
think that P has a reason to accept your principle. For, if P has a
reason to accept your principle, then the fact that steak is meat
could give P a reason not to eat steak even though he does not in
fact accept your principle. But if P has no reason to accept your
principle or a principle similar to it, it is not clear in what sense
the fact that steak is meat could provide him with a reason not to
eat steak.

So, when you say that P ought not to eat steak you imply that P
has a reason to accept your principle or a principle similar to it.
But Hare cannot always assume that this is so. As a post-Kantian
philosopher, Hare agrees with much of what Kant said but does
not think that there are reasons over and above mere consistency
that favor one choice of principles over various other possible
choices. Reason alone does not put such strong constraints on
your principles. So, as a post-Kantian philosopher, Hare cannot
say that P, who does not accept the principle, "Do not eat any
meat," necessarily has reasons to accept it. But if P does not have

any reasons to accept that principle, as is quite possible, given Hare's position, it cannot be said that P ought to accept that principle. For it would be inconsistent to say that P ought to accept the principle when he has no reasons to accept it. But then it cannot be said that P ought not to eat steak, if his principles give him no reason not to eat steak and he has no reasons to accept any principles that differ from those he now accepts.

Hare must allow that a certain case is possible, in which the speaker's basic principles conflict with the agent's. In such a case, Hare's theory allows the speaker to say that the agent ought to do a certain thing, even though doing that thing does not accord with the agent's own principles. Such a judgment implies that the agent has a reason to do that thing; and this can be so, in this situation, only if the agent has a reason to adopt a principle similar to the principle to which the speaker is appealing. But the whole point of Hare's variant of Kant's theory is that the agent cannot have reasons to adopt different principles unless there is some sort of incoherence or irrationality in his own principles. Since there need be no such incoherence or irrationality in the agent's principles, Hare's theory can lead a speaker into contradiction. For the theory tells the speaker that he may judge an agent on the basis of the speaker's principles, which judgment implies that the agent has reasons to accept the speaker's principles, although the whole point of Hare's theory is that the agent may well have no reasons to accept principles that differ from the principles he actually accepts.

Now, Hare could easily meet this objection by modifying his analysis in the following way. He could suppose that "P ought to do D" means something like "P's doing D is in accordance with the general moral principles to which I hereby subscribe and which P also accepts or at least has good reasons to accept." But this would mean that you cannot make a moral judgment using the moral "ought" about someone who does not accept the relevant principle and has no reason to accept it. And this may seem wrong too. For, as Kant observes, it seems that we can make such judgments about anyone, no matter what their moral principles are.

There are then two possibilities. One is that Hare's theory, even revised in the way suggested, simply does not work, so that we are left with Sartre's view that morality is no more than good faith and consistency. The other possibility is that something is wrong with our ordinary view that we can make moral "ought" judgments about anyone, no matter what their principles are. We have already considered in the last chapter that we might want to give up the idea that our moral principles are binding on all rational beings. As we saw there, this idea is itself a reflection of that aspect of our ordinary moral views that Kant described and that post-Kantian philosophers say we must abandon. We cannot have morality as it is ordinarily conceived. Perhaps all we can have is the substitute Hare provides, given the suggested revision of his theory. In that case, morality begins to acquire the character of principles that are accepted by a group of people. Our moral principles are binding only on those who share them or whose principles give them reasons to accept them.

A note on further reading

R. M. Hare's theory is developed in *The Language of Morals* (Oxford: Oxford University Press, 1952).

For a popular version of J. P. Sartre's view, see "Existentialism is a Humanism," in Walter Kaufmann, *Existentialism from Dostoevsky* to Sartre (New York: Meridian, 1956).

8 Custom and relativity

1. Internalism and externalism

Morality gives people reasons to do things. If an ethical theory is to be adequate, it must explain why this is so. Therefore, the ideal observer theory (for example) is defective in that it does not say why anyone has a reason to do what he ought morally to do. The theory says that someone ought morally to do something if and only if an ideal unbiased observer would approve of his doing it; but the theory does not say how the reactions of such a hypothetical unbiased ideal observer give a typically biased actual person a reason to do anything, because the theory does not say why anyone should care about the reactions of this imaginary person.

The objection to the ideal observer theory is an instance of the open question argument discussed in Chapter 2. The ideal observer theory is a form of ethical naturalism. Any naturalistic theory equates the remark "P ought morally to do D" with a remark of the form "P's doing D would have natural characterstics C." If we do not clearly care about an action's being C, it will be an open question for us whether someone ought to do something that has characteristics C, because we do care about what people ought morally to do.

It is true that we are not always motivated to do what we think is right. Sometimes we are tempted to do something else and sometimes we just do not care. But normally we do care about right and wrong and an ethical theory must somehow account for our concern. Ethical theories can be distinguished in terms of the different ways in which they try to explain this. Some say our concern is purely internal to our moral beliefs, whereas others say that it depends at least in part on external sanctions. For example, a divine law theory says that right and wrong derive from God's law, which He enforces with divine sanctions; in this view, we care about right and wrong because we care about whether we are going to go to Heaven or to Hell. Emotivism, on the other hand, tries to explain our concern with right and wrong by identifying the thought that something is right with one sort of concern and the thought that something is wrong with the opposite sort of concern. Emotivism takes moral concern to be purely internal to our moral beliefs, whereas a divine law theory holds that it derives in part from external sanctions. Emotivism is a kind of *internalism;* the divine law theory is a kind of *externalism.*

The main problem with internalism is that, as we have seen, it tends toward subjectivism, given the apparent facts of human psychology and the apparent limits of rationality. Different people appear to be able to adopt different moral principles without being irrational. There are limits of consistency, of course; and, at least according to Hare, not just any principles you might adopt will count as moral principles. For, according to Hare, you must not only intend to follow those principles yourself but must also intend to try to get others to follow them. But, even in Hare's view, different sets of moral principles are possible and, if one person's moral principles are different from another's, there is no sense in which the one person's set of moral principles can be said to be right and the other's wrong, apart from internal incoherence or inconsistency, except in the sense that a speaker can indicate agreement with one set and not with the other.

Subjectivism like this is counter-intuitive, because we are ordinarily inclined to suppose that a person's intentions, aims, goals, plans, and projects are one sort of thing and morality is another. We do not ordinarily suppose that right and wrong are determined by a particular individual's decisions and principles. We are inclined to think that morality has an external source, not an internal one.

Now, externalism takes it as essential to our concern for right and wrong that this concern should derive at least partly from some sort of external sanctions. The divine law theory says that these sanctions include withdrawal of God's love and punishment in Hell. It is sometimes even suggested that if someone does not believe in divine punishment and reward, he will not believe in an objective moral law at all; and furthermore, although he may believe in a subjective law he gives to himself, it is said that such a subjective law cannot be considered a moral law in any ordinary sense, since the person in question will be able to think of himself as free to act without objective moral constraints. "If God is dead, everything is permitted." But this line of thought assumes too quickly that the only possible external sanction for the moral law is divine retribution. The argument is better conceived as an argument for externalism: pure internalism makes morality out to be too subjective; our ordinary conception of morality is of something with a more objective nature. A person normally supposes that morality transcends the principles that he himself happens to have adopted; if we were to come to believe that Hare was really right and that morality was nothing over and above a particular person's principles, we would have to conclude that there are no moral constraints of the sort we ordinarily believe in. "If externalism is dead, everything is permitted."

2. Social custom and morality

Let us suppose, then, that morality does depend, at least in part, on external sanctions. If these are not divine, they must be human; that is, they must be social. Morality must, then depend essentially on some sort of social law enforced by custom and social pressure. Of course, morality is not to be identified with legality; we must not say that the moral law is the same as the law the *government* enforces. On the other hand, we do not have to assume that the dividing line between morality and (civil and criminal) law is a sharp one. Just what the relation is between law and morality is a crucial question for any social custom theory of morality; but it is a question that can be put to one side for the present. We can define social custom theories loosely as theories that say that morality derives from the rules or customs that society enforces in a certain way, a way that may be specified differently in different theories.

A successful social custom theory in this sense would have two obvious prima facie advantages over pure internalism. First, it would account for our intuitive feeling that morality has a source that is external to the principles a particular person happens to have adopted. Right and wrong would turn out not to be matters of personal choice. Second, the theory would begin to explain why morality has the particular content we normally suppose it has. For example, we normally suppose that there are moral restrictions on stealing, lying, and cheating and that there are moral duties to be honest, to help others, and to show gratitude when you are helped. It is obvious that society has an interest in such restrictions and duties. Rules against stealing, lying, and cheating and in favor of helping, of being honest, and so forth, are in the general interest. Quite apart from any assumptions about a prior morality, we can understand why there might be social pressure to act in accordance with these rules, because this pressure would serve a social function. If we can assume that morality derives from the social enforcement of certain customs, we can begin to explain why there are the sorts of moral principles we think there are. On the other hand, if we assume that morality is simply a reflection of individual decisions, we cannot offer such an explanation (although we might offer an evolutionary explanation in that case—the tendency to develop social values promotes the survival of people who are born with that tendency).

In a social custom theory of morality, then, the enforcement of custom is basic to morality. Morality is constituted by the rules, whatever they are, that society enforces. There is no prior morality. If society were to enforce different rules, what is right and what is wrong would change.

But we must not oversimplify. The theory does not simply identify something's being wrong with there being social pressure against it. That would clearly be inadequate. To say that morality derives from rules that are socially enforced is not to say that whatever is customary is right. Slavery, for example, can be wrong, according to a social custom theory, even if it is customary and there is no social pressure against it. For, even when slavery itself is customary, it can conflict with other customs that are socially enforced; this conflict may not be recognized by the members of society because of ignorance of fact, stupidity, and self-deception. According to the social custom theory, if slavery is wrong in the society, it is wrong because of the rules that are socially enforced with respect to people who are not slaves. These rules may really apply to everyone and not just to non-slaves, even though members of the society do not recognize this because they falsely believe that there is an important relevant difference between slaves and other people and therefore think of the slaves as, say, beasts of burden rather than as people.

In the case of social rules, as in the case of personal rules, there can be more basic and less basic principles. Given socially enforced basic principles and certain factual beliefs, the members of society will enforce other principles that they derive from the basic principles and factual assumptions. If their factual assumptions are mistaken, their derivative principles will be incorrect even from their own point of view. A social custom theory of morality can therefore suppose that morality derives from principles that are socially enforced without having to assume that what is socially enforced is always right. Such a theory of morality is not committed to saying that, if there is a custom of slavery, slavery must be right. It is only committed to saying that, if slavery is wrong, it is wrong with reference to some custom or other that is socially enforced.

This does mean that, if there were no social constraints at all, there would be nothing wrong with slavery, since there would in that case be nothing wrong with anything according to the social custom theory. In a "state of nature" nothing would be right or wrong, because no rules would be socially enforced. We must now consider how plausible this is. We must imagine people living quite separate lives, never cooperating in any sort of semipermanent way, so that there is no such thing as a society even on a small scale. Then we must ask ourselves whether we think that there would still be right and wrong in such a state of nature.

Now, many people find, when they consider this carefully, they do think that, even in a state of nature, you should not kill other people or harm them in any way (except in self-defense, etc.); you should not steal from them; you should not try to mislead them; you should try to help them if they need help. Other people feel that a state of nature would be more like a condition of all-out war of each one against the others in which moral constraints would play no real role. If the first group of people are right, no social custom theory of morality can be adequate to our ordinary conception of morality. But it is difficult to get a clear picture of what a state of nature would be like; so it is not easy to be sure whether you think that moral constraints would apply in such a state. Furthermore, it is certainly not *clearly* essential to our usual conception of morality that moral constraints should apply in a state of nature. Therefore, it is useful to consider whether there are other considerations relevant to the evaluation of social custom theories of morality.

3. Relativism again

One possible difficulty with such a theory is its relativistic character. The basic rules that are socially enforced in one society may differ from the basic rules enforced in another. So, according to a social custom theory, what is right and what is wrong will not always be the same in different societies. Yet our ordinary conception of morality may not appear to allow this sort of relativity.

In considering differences in the moral codes of different societies, it is useful to distinguish three different cases: (a) cases concerning which we are inclined to say, "When in Rome, do as the Romans do," (b) cases like the slavery example in which we think that, even with respect to their own morality, the members of the society ought not to act as they customarily do, and (c) cases that do not fall under either (a) or (b).

In the first of these categories fall social conventions of politeness, deference, and etiquette. Although these conventions vary greatly from one society to another, that does not particularly disturb us. These conventions have a social function: they help smooth relations with others, making certain activities more predictable and easier to participate in; they make it possible for one to relax in various social situations; and they reduce confusion. But it does not matter very much exactly what the conventions are, as long as there are some rules. These rules are therefore very much like linguistic conventions or rules of the road.

In the second category are conventions having to do with marriage and the family, as well as conventions concerning what is to count as sexual perversion, what attitudes are appropriate as regards homosexuality or premarital sexual relations, and so forth.

Questions of abortion, infanticide, and cruelty to animals are also in this category. We are not inclined to think that the conventions of a society with respect to these matters can determine, at
least in any simple way, what is right and wrong. Just as slavery
is unjust to slaves, so too the social institution of marriage and the
family as it exists in a given society may be unfair to the women
of that society. This may also be true for the customs of that society regarding perversion, homosexuality, infanticide, abortion,
and cruelty to animals. In these cases, we do not feel, "When in
Rome, do as the Romans do." An American married couple
traveling to an Arab country will not feel that the husband
should treat his wife in accordance with local custom.

Still, these cases can be classed together because of the way in
which they resemble the slavery example. It may be that the
socially enforced rules for relations between men are the rules
with reference to which the treatment of women is wrong in the
society, just as the rules that are enforced with respect to non-
slaves may be the rules with reference to which slavery is wrong.
For it may be that the treatment of women is based on false
assumptions about differences between men and women. Similarly, social restrictions on homosexual behavior may derive
from false beliefs about homosexuality. Again, our treatment of
animals may be based on false beliefs about the differences
between people and animals.

I do not mean to suggest that we will have no difficulty using a
social custom theory to account for our moral views with respect
to these examples. But it is not clear that such a theory cannot
account for our views. Therefore, it is useful to consider examples of cases that fall into the third category, cases for which
objectionable social practices do not seem to based on mistakes
about the facts of a case.

Consider a society in which cannibalism is permitted. In that
society, there is no rule against eating human flesh, as there is in
our society. To keep matters simple, we should not suppose that
they actually raise humans expressly for the purpose of eating
human flesh, as we raise certain animals. Nor should we suppose
that they hunt people in the way in which our ancestors used to
hunt animals. The people that are eaten, then, are people who
have died natural or accidental deaths, people who have been
legitimately executed as criminals, and people who have been

killed in wars. In our society, we think that it is wrong to eat human flesh even in these cases. The issue is whether it is wrong for those in the cannibal society to do so.

Here again, our intuitions are unclear and conflicting. On the one hand, we have some inclination to think that, when cannibalism is a custom of a society, the members of that society who eat human flesh cannot be blamed for doing so. We feel uncomfortable about saying that it is morally wrong *of them* to eat human flesh. On the other hand, we also believe that their practice is objectionable. And, certainly, if one of us were to visit that society, it would be wrong of him to engage in that practice. This is therefore definitely not for us a case of "When in Rome, do as the Romans do."

To take a different example, suppose that there is another society in which people recognize an obligation not to injure each other but not a duty to help each other when help is needed. When someone has an accident or gets sick, no one in this second society assumes he has any reason to help that person get to the doctor, and it never occurs to one of these people to warn you if there is a wasp on your hamburger. The question, then, is whether, despite this lack of a socially enforced rule, the members of this society ought morally to help one another when they can do so at little or no cost to themselves. And again this is a hard problem to solve intuitively. We are inclined to think, on the one hand, that there is something wrong with the rules of the society. For we suppose that there ought to be a socially enforced rule of mutual aid. But that is not to say that in the absence of such a rule the members of the society still have a moral duty to help someone in distress, and, given the social practices of the society, it is not obvious that anyone in it can be blamed for not helping others.

Furthermore, it is not obvious that if you were to visit that society and were to see someone in need of help, which you but no one else could provide, you would have any duty to help. For, if the situation were reversed, he would not suppose that he had any reason to help you; and it is not clear that you are obligated to help someone whom you know would not help you if the situation were reversed. There would not be anything wrong with helping him; indeed, it would be nice of you to do so; it would be a good thing. But that is not to say that you would have any moral duty or obligation to help him.

So, when we consider the most crucial cases for a social custom theory of morality, we find it hard to decide whether the theory agrees or conflicts with our intuitions. This is in part due to the vagueness of such theories as we have so far described them and in part due to the complexity of our reactions. In the next chapter we will consider a more precise theory that supposes that morality rests on a tacit convention among the members of society, and we will try to sort out the different aspects of our intuitions about these cases.

A note on further reading

William Frankena contrasts internalism with externalism in "Obligation and Motivation in Recent Moral Philosophy," in A. I. Melden, *Essays in Moral Philosophy* (Seattle: University of Washington Press, 1956).

There is a useful collection edited by John Ladd, *Relativism* (Belmont, Calif.: Wadsworth, 1973).

IV

Reasons and conventions

9 Convention

1. Moral conventions

Hume says that some, but not all, aspects of morality rest on "convention." There is a convention in Hume's sense when each of a number of people adheres to certain principles so that each of the others will also adhere to these principles. I adhere to the principles in my dealings with the others because I benefit from their adherence to these principles in their dealings with me and because I think that they will stop adhering to these principles in their dealings with me unless I continue to adhere to the principles in my dealings with them. For example, two farmers have a convention of helping each other till their fields. Farmer A helps farmer B till his fields so that when it comes time to till farmer A's fields, farmer B will help farmer A. Each farmer benefits from this practice, which depends upon their expectation that the other will continue it.

Hume mentions other conventions of this sort, for example those that give rise to the institutions of money. Certain pieces of paper can be traded for goods only because they will be accepted in turn by others in exchange for their goods. The conventions of language provide another example, one which indicates that conventions may be extremely subtle and even impossible for an ordinary person to describe in any precise and explicit way.

Conventions are reached through a process of implicit bargaining and mutual adjustment. Two people rowing a boat will adjust their actions with respect to each other so that they pull at the same time. It does not matter what their rate is, as long as both row at the same rate. If one tries to row more quickly and the other tries to row more slowly, some sort of compromise will have to be reached.

Among the most important conventions, according to Hume, are those having to do with property. It is useful to each person that there should be a system of security regarding possessions. This system is entirely conventional; and until it develops, there is no such thing as property. Another important convention is the one that makes possible explicit contracts and promises. The convention is that, by using a certain form of words (or other sign), a person binds himself to do what he says he will do. The obligation to keep your promises therefore itself derives from a prior convention, according to Hume.

Hume says that the original motive to observe conventions is "natural" rather than moral, by which he means that it is a self-interested motive. Initially, each person continues to adhere to the conventional principles in his dealings with others so that they will continue to do so in their dealings with him. Eventually habits develop. Action in accordance with those principles becomes relatively automatic; it would be hard to change. Obligations based on those principles come to seem natural and obvious. According to Hume, these "natural" obligations will strike us as moral as soon as we reflect sympathetically on the usefulness of the relevant conventions to human society. For, as you will recall, Hume accepts a kind of ideal observer theory. In his view, moral judgments express feelings based on sympathy.

Hume himself does not think that everything about morality is conventional, although he thinks that much is. He holds that sympathy can lead us to approve or disapprove of some things apart from prior conventions—for example, we will approve of kindness to others even in a state of nature—and, in Hume's view, this is moral approval. But he would probably agree that moral *obligations* and *duties* depend on convention; in any event, I will assume in what follows that this is part of Hume's theory.

A more extreme theory than Hume's would treat every aspect of morality as conventional. For example, when Hume believes that a weak sympathy for others is built into people, it might be supposed instead that sympathy itself derives from a convention whereby people tacitly agree to respect each other at least to the extent of trying to feel sympathy for others. But we do not need to decide between Hume's theory and this more extreme version.

Hume's tacit convention theory of morality is a more specific version of the social custom theory. It has a number of advantages. For one thing, it provides a more specific account of the way in which morality involves social utility: certain rules are conventionally adopted because each person benefits from everyone else acting in accordance with those rules. We therefore expect rules to be adopted if they promote social utility in the sense that they are beneficial to all.

To take another example, as noted in the last chapter we do not normally assume that you are obligated to help someone when you know that he would not help you if the situation were reversed; we feel that to help such a person would be to do something that is above and beyond the call of duty, a generous act rather than something you are obligated to do. But this is just what we would expect given Hume's theory. There are reasons of self-interest for people to adopt a convention of *mutual* aid, but no obvious reasons of this sort to extend this convention to aid those who do not participate in the convention. So, given Hume's theory, we would not expect an obligation or duty to help the person who would not help you. On the other hand, sympathy would lead an observer to approve of your helping this person; so, given Hume's theory, it would be a good thing if you were to help him even though you are not obligated to do so.

We noted in the previous chapter our reluctance to blame cannibals for eating human flesh, despite our abhorrence of their doing so and our view that it would be wrong for any of us to do so while visiting a society that practiced cannibalism. Given Hume's theory we might explain our own aversion to the eating of human flesh in the following way. We have a tacit convention in our society that we will respect each other as people. We will, in Kant's phrase, "treat people as ends," as if they were sacred and possessed a special kind of dignity. Furthermore, there are various conventional forms in which we have come to express our respect and we have therefore come to see it as demeaning to human dignity if persons are not treated according to these conventions. For example, if someone dies, we think it appropriate to hold a funeral and bury the body or perhaps cremate it. Given our current conventions, we will not eat the body. To do that would strike us as an insult to the memory of the person who has died. It would indicate a lack of respect for persons as persons. Our respect for people and our conventional habits of expressing that respect lead us automatically to reject the idea that we could eat human flesh; indeed, we have come to find the very idea disgusting.

Our reactions to the cannibals are complicated, however, because two moralities are relevant, theirs and ours. In judging the situation, we can simply appeal to our own morality: "Eating people is wrong!" But in judging the cannibals themselves, we must take their morality into account. We cannot simply blame them for what they do, because their moral understanding is not the same as ours. They see nothing wrong with eating people; and there is no obvious reason why they should. This makes it difficult for us to judge that it is wrong *of them* to eat human flesh. We do not feel comfortable in judging the cannibals themselves to be wrong. It does not seem right to say that each of them ought morally not to eat human flesh or that each of them has a moral duty or obligation not to do so. At best we might say that it ought not to be the case that they eat human flesh; but as we have seen before that is not the same sort of judgment at all. From our own point of view we can judge their acts and their situation, even their society and morality; but we cannot, it seems, judge *them*.

This explanation is related to a point mentioned in Chapter 7. We are inclined to suppose that a person ought morally not to have done a particular thing only if we can also assume that he had a reason not to do it. We could not suppose that the cannibals ought morally not to eat human flesh unless we also supposed that they have a reason not to eat human flesh. The trouble is that we are presently assuming that they have no such reason, because their morality is not the same as ours. Given this assumption, we can make certain moral or evaluative judgments about the cannibals; for example, we can call them "ignorant savages." But we cannot correctly say of them that they are morally wrong to eat human flesh or that they ought morally not to do it.

2. Judging outsiders

Now, it is very difficult to get a clear grasp on such examples just because it is not always clear when someone has a reason to do something and when he does not. To take a very different sort of example, Hitler, who had millions of people killed, was an extraordinarily evil man. In some sense we can say that he ought not to have killed those people and that what he did was wrong. Yet the following remarks are weak and even in some way odd: "It was wrong of Hitler to have ordered the extermination of the Jews." "Hitler ought morally not to have ordered the extermination of the Jews."

One might suppose that it is the enormity of Hitler's crime against humanity that makes such remarks seem too weak. He killed so many people; it would have been wrong of him to have killed only one. To say simply that it was wrong of him to have ordered the extermination of the Jews suggests that it was *only* wrong—that it is wrong only in the way in which murder is wrong. And, given what Hitler did, that is as if one were to say that it was *naughty* of Hitler to have ordered the extermination of the Jews.

This explanation, however, is not completely satisfactory. First of all, there are things we can say about Hitler without the same sort of oddity. Although it would be odd to say that it was wrong of Hitler to have acted as he did, it is not equally odd to say that what Hitler did was wrong. Similarly, there is no oddness in the remark, "What Hitler did ought never to have happened." That is not odd in the way that it is odd to say, "Hitler ought morally not to have ordered the extermination of the Jews." But, if the enormity of his crime makes the one remark odd, why doesn't it make the other remark as odd?

Another reason for doubting that the enormity of the crime, by itself, is the reason for the oddness in certain of these judgments is that we can make these very judgments about someone who has committed an equally enormous crime, at least if enormity is measured in numbers of people killed. For example, Stalin was also a mass murderer who ordered the purges of the thirties knowing that millions of people would be killed. Yet it is possible to think that Stalin was really only trying to do the right thing, that he hated the prospect of the purges, that he was however also alarmed at the consequences of not ordering the purges because he was afraid that the revolution was in danger of collapse. He found himself faced with a terrible choice and he opted for what he took to be the lesser of two evils. I am not suggesting that this is the truth about Stalin; it probably is not. I mean only that this is a possible view of Stalin. Of course, even someone taking such a sympathetic view of Stalin can suppose that Stalin was terribly mistaken. To take this view of Stalin is certainly not to condone Stalin's actions. It can never be right to order the deaths of millions of people like that, no matter what you hope to gain. Indeed, taking this view of Stalin, it is natural to say that it was wrong of Stalin to have ordered the purges; Stalin was morally wrong to have done so. The interesting question, then, is why is it not odd to say this about Stalin in the way that it is odd to say the same thing about Hitler. It cannot be the vast numbers of people killed that makes a difference, since vast numbers were killed by both men. And certainly the judgment that it was wrong of Stalin to have ordered the purges is not the judgment that it was *naughty* of him to have done so. Why then does it seem that if you say that it was wrong of Hitler to have done what he did you are saying something as odd and ridiculous as if you had said that it was naughty of Hitler to have done that.

Part of the answer has to do with our conception of the attitudes that we think Hitler and Stalin took toward their crimes, with the moral principles we think of them accepting, with our views of what they considered to be reasons for action. Hitler's attitude was in this respect much more extreme than Stalin's. Hitler is farther from us than Stalin is (or as Stalin is imagined to be in the view of him that I have sketched). Hitler is beyond the pale in a way that Stalin was not. Hitler was not just immoral, he was amoral, he was evil. Stalin was terrible and also, perhaps, evil; but he was not wholly beyond the reaches of morality as I have imagined him. We cannot but think of Hitler as beyond the reaches of morality or at least that part of morality that we invoke in judging him to be an evil man.

In saying that it was wrong of Hitler to have ordered the extermination of the Jews we would be saying that Hitler had a reason (every reason in the world) not to do what he did. But what is horrible about someone who did what he did is that he could not have had such a reason. If he was willing to exterminate a whole people, there was no reason for him not to do so: that is just what is so terrible about him. That is why it sounds too weak to say that it was wrong of him to do what he did. It suggests that he had a reason not to act as he did and we feel that any man who could have done what Hitler did must be the sort of man who would not have had a reason not to do it. Such a man is evil rather than wrong.

This is why it is odd to say that it was wrong of Hitler to have acted as he did but it is not odd to say that Hitler's act was wrong. The judgment that Hitler's act was wrong and the judgment that it never ought to have happened do not imply that Hitler had a reason not to do what he did. The fact that we feel that Hitler was not the sort of person who could have had such a reason does not undermine judgments of his *acts* in the way that it undermines certain judgments about *him*.

All this is explicable in Hume's tacit convention theory. Hitler, like the cannibals, is outside our morality, although in a different direction. We can judge his acts with reference to our morality, but not Hitler himself, since that would imply that he was someone who acknowledged the moral standards we use to judge him. To say, "It was wrong of Hitler" or "Hitler ought morally not to have done it" would imply that Hitler accepted the relevant moral conventions. But his actions show that he does not accept those conventions. He is therefore beyond the pale and an enemy of humanity.

There are other examples that confirm the same point. Consider judgments that we might make about Martians who felt no concern for us. Suppose that these Martians would not be deterred from a given course of action simply by the reflection that that course of action would harm some human being. These Martians would not treat such a consideration as any sort of reason. For them, the consideration would simply not tell against that course of action at all. In that case, we cannot say that it would be morally wrong of the Martians to harm us.

This is to disagree with Kant, who would say that, since a Martian is a rational being, it has a reason not to harm any of us, because we too are rational beings. "The Martian would not agree to our harming it; so how can it agree to its harming us?" Kant believes that reflection of this sort can provide the Martian with motivation not to harm us. If Kant were right, there would be no need for moral conventions. We could make do with pure practical reason alone.

Now a defender of Hume's tacit convention theory will assume, plausibly, that Kant is mistaken about the powers of pure practical reason. When we first come across the Martians, they may well have no reason to be concerned about us at all, and, in that case, there are no moral constraints on them in their dealings with us. If they harm us, that is not a matter of morality or immorality, although it may well be a matter of war between the planets. If it turns out that there is no way for us to harm the Martians, so that they do not need to be concerned about us even for reasons of self-interest, then a morality that encompasses us and them may never develop.

On the other hand, if a conflict develops that is in neither their interest nor ours, we and they may try to arrive at conventions that would reduce or eliminate this sort of conflict. For example, we and they might adopt a convention of respect for each other as rational beings that would involve, among other things, trying to avoid actions that would harm other rational beings. In that case, there would be a morality encompassing us and them.

This is how a morality would arise from a state of nature, according to a tacit convention theory. Before any conventions were established, there would be no such thing as right and wrong; it would not make sense to judge what people morally ought or ought not to do. But once a group of people developed conventional patterns of action in order to avoid conflicts with each other, their actions could be judged with reference to those conventions. People who remained outside the relevant group and still in a state of nature could, however, not be so judged.

3. Conventional aspects of morality

One reason for thinking that morality has arisen like this, as the result of convention, is that certain elements in our actual moral views seem to reflect what would be the result of implicit bargaining and mutual adjustments between people of different powers and resources. For example, consider a point I have alluded to several times. In our morality, harming someone is thought to be much worse than helping someone. That is why we suppose that a doctor cannot cut up one patient in order to save five other patients by distributing the one patient's organs according to need. Now, this general principle about harming and not helping may seem irrational and unmotivated, but it makes sense if we suppose that our moral views derive from a tacit convention that arose among people of different wealth, status, and power. For, whereas everyone would benefit equally from a conventional practice of trying not to harm each other, some people would benefit considerably more than others from a convention to help those who needed help. The rich and powerful do not need much help and are often in the best position to give it; so, if a strong principle of mutual aid were adopted, they would gain little and lose a great deal, because they would end up doing most of the helping and would receive little in return. On the other hand, the poor and weak might refuse to agree to a principle of noninterference or noninjury unless they also reached some agreement on mutual aid. We would therefore expect a compromise, as in our example of the two rowers who arrive at a rate intermediate between the rates that each prefers to row at. In the present case, the expected compromise would involve a strong principle of noninjury and a much weaker principle of mutual aid—which is just what we now have. If our moral principles were not in this way a result of bargaining and adjustment, it would be hard to see why we would suppose that there is this moral difference between harming and not helping; and it would be hard to understand how our moral principles could be the result of bargaining and adjustment in this way unless they were derived from some sort of convention in Hume's sense. So, this aspect of our moral views is evidence in favor of Hume's tacit convention theory.

Now, it is important that Hume's theory is an *actual* convention theory. Duties and obligations are seen as deriving from actual, not hypothetical, conventions. Hume's theory is therefore to be distinguished from hypothetical agreement theories that say that the correct moral rules are those that people *would* agree to under certain conditons of equality. Hume's explanation of moral motivation requires his actual convention theory and does not work on any sort of hypothetical agreement theory. Hume says that we act morally first out of self-interest and then out of a habit of following certain conventional rules. We cannot in the same way explain why someone would be motivated to adhere to principles he *would have* agreed to adhere to in a position of equality.

Furthermore, the suggested explanation of the moral

difference we recognize between harming and not helping depends on the assumption that our morality rests on an actual convention among people of different powers and resources. It is not easy to see how this aspect of our moral views could be explained by assuming that obligations depend on what we *would* agree to in a position of equality. For, in such a position, it seems likely that we would not agree to our present moral principles.

4. The tacit convention theory and Kant's theory

Finally, it should also be observed that the tacit convention theory follows important aspects of Kant's theory, even though it rejects one of Kant's key ideas. Kant argued that we must think of the principles of morality as principles that each of us legislates for himself and for others, whom we perceive as also legislating the same principles. It is this second part that distinguishes Kant's theory from Hare's. Hare says that each person thinks of the principles of morality as principles that he legislates for himself and for others, but Hare does not assume that a person must think of the others as legislating the same principles. And this led to a difficulty for Hare (I argued) when we considered making judgments about someone who does not share the relevant principles. The tacit convention theory, like Kant's theory, sees moral principles as principles for which the source is both internal and external. They are principles legislated by others and by yourself. They represent the principles of a general will. Kant was wrong in thinking that these principles are determined by reason alone and therefore wrong to assume that they were universal. Nevertheless he was right to emphasize their objectivity and interpersonal character. The private principles of one person, which that person does not take to be shared by others, do not represent a normal case of moral principles. At best, they represent a limiting case. Morality is essentially social.

The tacit convention theory of morality is therefore not a version of pure externalism. It is a combination: internalism plus externalism. The principles that apply to you, according to this theory, are not simply whatever principles are conventionally accepted by the surrounding group; you must accept the conventions too. Otherwise they could not give you reasons to do things, and judgment about what you ought morally to do or about what it would be right or wrong of you to do could not be made with reference to those conventions. An amoral person can exist in the midst of others who share a common morality. But such a person can no more be judged in terms of other people's principles than can Hitler or the cannibals. If a Martian who does not care about human life decides to live in our midst but does not see any reason to accept our conventions, we cannot say correctly that the Martian is morally obligated not to harm us (although we can judge that it would be a bad thing if the Martians were to harm us). Similarly, it would be a misuse of language to say of hardened professional criminals that it is morally wrong of them to steal from others or that they ought morally not to kill people. Since they do not share our conventions, they have no moral reasons to refrain from stealing from us or killing us. (On the other hand, we can judge them enemies of society and can say that they ought to be hunted down and put into prison.)

Moralities are social. The are defined by the conventions of groups. But you belong to more than one group, and different groups have different conventions. Which conventions determine your moral obligations? They all do. Since you belong to a number of different groups, you are subject to a number of different moralities—the morality of your family, perhaps your school, a professional morality (your "business ethics"), the morality of your neighborhood, the various moralities of various groups of friends, the morality of your country, and finally, perhaps, a limited morality you share with most of humanity. These moralities will sometimes be in conflict, and give rise to a tragic situation in which you are faced with a conflict of loyalties. In that case, there is no clear moral solution to your problem. You must choose the group which is most important to you and act on its conventions.

There is a limiting case of morality in which the relevant "group" contains only one person. In that case, a person will be able to say he has certain moral obligations deriving from his personal principles and will not judge others to be similarly obligated (by his principles). For example, a pacifist may think that he morally ought not to participate in wars, although he will not make the same judgment about other persons. He will not say that it is wrong of them to participate, although he will certainly think that it is bad for everyone that they engage in wars. And there are many other cases in which a person imposes moral obligations and duties on himself without supposing that other persons are similarly obligated.

This represents a limiting case of morality rather than a central case (even though it may be a common case) because we normally think of a morality as a set of principles that can be used to judge more than one person and because, as we saw in Chapter 8, we think of morality as imposing external constraints on someone. Without objective external constraints, there would be no such thing as morality, as we ordinarily understand it, even if people adhered to their own personal principles. If there were only individual moralities, only sets of personal principles and no group conventions, morality as we normally think of it would not yet exist.

A note on further reading

Hume's account of convention appears in his *Treatise on Human Nature*, Book 3, Part 2, Section 2.

There is an exhaustive treatment of this and related notions in David Lewis, *Convention* (Cambridge, Mass.: Harvard University Press, 1969).

For further discussion see Gilbert Harman, "Moral Relativism Defended," in *Philosophical Review*, Vol. 74 (1975).

10 Reasons

1. Logic and reasons

As we have seen, a number of ethical theories take the correctness of a moral "ought" judgment to depend on how that judgment is related to certain practical principles, although the theories differ concerning what they take the relevant principles to be. Kant, for example, says that the relevant principles are the universal principles of pure practical reason. Hare says that they are whatever universalizable principles the person making the "ought" judgment subscribes to. Sartre says that they are the principles that are accepted by the person about whom the "ought" judgment is made. In the convention theory, the relevant principles are those conventionally accepted by the members of some contextually indicated group that includes both the person being judged and the person making the judgment.

Such theories also differ in what they say about the required relation between practical principles and moral judgment. For example, Hare's theory is that this is a logical relation that is to be explained within a logic of imperatives. An alternative and more plausible idea is that the relevant relation is a weaker nonlogical relation of the sort that holds between reasons and the judgment for which the reasons are reasons.

According to Hare, the relevant practical principles can be formulated as general imperatives; and an "ought" judgment is correct, relative to a set of general imperatives. if a corresponding imperative follows logically from the set of general imperatives taken together with true factual assumptions. For example, suppose that the person making the judgment accepts the principle, "Anyone, give someone what you owe him if you can and he asks for it back!" Suppose also that the facts include (a) that Jones owes Smith ten dollars, (b) that Smith has asked for the money back, and (c) that Jones can now pay back the money. Hare believes that from these suppositions we can derive the imperative "Jones, pay Smith the ten dollars you owe him!" So, in Hare's view, the judgment that Jones ought to pay Smith the ten dollars he owes him is correct, in relation to that general principle, given those facts. This idea, about the required relation between particular "ought" judgment and general principles, could also be accepted in a Kantian, Sartrean, or convention theory of morality. Any of these theories could say that a moral "ought" judgment is correct if, and only if, it is a logical consequence of the relevant practical principles and the facts of the case. The difference between the theories would then have to do with the nature of the relevant principles and not with the required relation between principles and particular "ought" judgments.

But the idea that there must be this sort of logical relation between principles and particular judgments is not very plausible. For one thing, it implies that the relevant principles are so detailed that they determine logically exactly what we are to do in every possible circumstance. There is an air of unreality to the idea that moral principles have this sort of precision.

There is, furthermore, a looseness to "ought" judgments that this idea fails to express. "P ought to do D" is not the only sort of judgment we want to make relative to the relevant practical principles. We also want to be able to make such judgments as "It would be good of P to do D," "It would be wrong of P not to do D," "P might do D," "P must do D." These judgments do not all have the same meaning. Some are appropriate where others are not. Hare's theory on its face seems more appropriate for the judgment "P must do D" than for "P ought to do D." For, to say that P ought to do D is not necessarily to say that P's doing D is absolutely required. It would be better, if that is what is meant, to say that P has to do D or that it would be wrong of P not to do D. We can assume that P ought to do D without assuming that he absolutely must do D or even that it would be wrong of him not to do D. To say that P ought to do D, on the other hand, is stronger than to say simply that it would be good of P if he were to do D.

2. A good-reasons analysis

This suggests an alternative theory according to which the relevant practical principles do not have the sort of legalistic precision required for Hare's theory to work. In this alternative theory, the relevant principles commit us not so much to particular actions in particular circumstances as to certain general aims and goals. We are to respect others; we are to try not to harm them; if there is no great cost to ourselves involved, we are to try to help those who need help; and so forth. There are also principles regarding duties and divisions of responsibilities, e.g., within families—parents are to be responsible for the education and well-being of their children, and so forth. In this theory, the relevant moral principles are not precise enough to allow us to determine what someone ought to do, if this has to be determined logically in the way that Hare suggests, since we cannot *deduce* what ought to be done, given the facts.

Still, in this alternative theory, as in Hare's theory, to accept principles as practical principles is to be motivated to act in certain ways. It is to have certain goals and ends in addition to the goals and ends you would have if you had not accepted those principles. And, just as your other goals, ends, desires, and plans can give you reasons to do things, so too can the goals and ends that you have as the result of accepting the conventions of society, for example. But, to say that these principles give you reasons to do things is not just to say that these principles logically imply certain imperatives. The relation of reasons is weaker than, or at least different from, the relation of logical implication via a logic of imperatives. It is this less precise relation of reasons that, in this theory, correctly expresses the connection between the relevant practical principles and particular "ought" judgments that are correct, in relation to those principles, given the facts.

In this theory, then, to say that P ought to do D is to say that P has sufficient reasons to do D that are stronger than the reasons he has to do something else. If what you mean is that P morally ought to do D, you mean that P has sufficient *moral* reasons to do D that are stronger than the reasons he has to do something else. In other words, given the relevant practical principles, for example, the principles that P accepts as the conventions of society, P has sufficient reasons deriving from those principles for doing D, etc.

The relevant reasons can be of varying strengths, which accounts for the various judgments that might be made: "P ought to do D," "D is the best thing P can do," "P must do D," "P may do D," and so forth. For example, given that P intends to adhere to certain principles and given the facts, it may be that there are good reasons for P to do D yet it would not at all be a mistake for P not to do D. In that case, it may not be true that P ought to do D although it would be good of P to do D. On the other hand, if, given P's intention to adhere to those principles and given the facts, it would be a mistake for P not to do D, P ought to do D. And, if it would be irrational for P not to do D, given that he really does intend to adhere to those principles, he must do D. Not doing D in such a case would be incompatible with continuing to intend to adhere to those principles. To say, relative to certain principles, that P must do D is to say that, if P does not do D, that will show that he does not in fact seriously intend to adhere to those principles. Finally, to say that P may do D or might do D relative to certain practical principles is to say that P's acceptance of those principles does not make it irrational for him to do D.

This kind of theory is sometimes called a "good-reasons analysis" of moral "ought" judgments and related moral judgments. In this theory, such judgments say something about the moral reasons a person has for doing something. A similar analysis would be inappropriate for other categories of moral judgment, such as the judgment that P is morally evil in doing D, since such judgments do not similarly depend on assumptions about P's reasons to do things.

Good-reasons analyses can also be given for other senses of "ought" and related words like "may" and "must." Recall that the word "ought" appears to have at least four different meanings. In additon to the moral "ought" we have been discussing, there is the simple "ought" of rationality, as when we say that the bank robber ought to use the rear door; the evaluative "ought," as in "There ought to be more love in the world"; and the "ought" of expectation, as in "The train ought to be here in three minutes." Corresponding to these different senses of "ought" are different senses of "must" and "may." There is, for example, a "must" of expectation, as when we say, "The train must have arrived by now," and there is a "may" or "might" of expectation, as when we say, "The train may arrive in a few minutes," or "The train might have arrived at noon; I'm not sure." Similarly, there are a "must," a "may," and a "might" of evaluation and also of simple rationality. We say, for example, "The hurricane mustn't hit Miami" or "The bank robber must cut the alarm wires if he is to escape detection."

Good-reasons analyses, when they are suitably modified, are appropriate to these different cases. In the case of the "ought," "must," and "may" of expectation, what is relevant are reasons of belief. To say that the train ought to be here soon is to say that there are good reasons to think that the train will be here soon. To say that the train must have arrived by noon is to say that the reasons for thinking this are conclusive. To say that the train may not have arrived at all is to say that it is not incompatible with the reasons we currently have to suppose that the train has not arrived at all. Similarly, to say that the hurricane mustn't hit Miami is to say that there are overwhelming reasons to hope that the hurricane will not hit Miami. To say that there ought to be more love in the world is to say that there are reasons for wishing that there was more love in the world. To say that the bank robber ought to use the back door is to say that he has good reasons to use it. To say that he must cut the alarm wires is to say that it would be irrational for him not to, given his ends and given the facts.

3. Prima-facie "oughts"

One advantage of such a good-reasons analysis is that it allows us to account for various uses of "ought," "may," and "must." Another is that the good-reasons analysis helps explicate an aspect of our use of "ought" that was emphasized by the English philosopher W. D. Ross (1877–1970), who argued that there were two moral "oughts," a prima-facie "ought" and an all-things-considered "ought." Ross argued that, if we try to state our moral principles using the word "ought," we must use what he calls the prima-facie "ought." For example, we say, "You ought to keep your promises," "You ought to tell the truth," "You ought not to injure others," "You ought to help those in need," and so forth. But we do not suppose that these principles are absolute. We do not suppose that you ought to keep every promise; we allow that there are circumstances in which you may break a promise—indeed there are circumstances in which you ought to break a promise. The same is true of other moral principles. "All moral principles have exceptions."

Hare's reaction to this point is to assume that our moral principles are really much more complicated. For Hare, the exceptions are built into the moral principles. But Ross used a different approach. According to him, a principle like, "You ought to keep your promises," is true as it stands; but this principle does not mean that there are no situations in which you may break your promise. According to Ross, the "ought" used in stating this principle is the prima-facie "ought." What is meant by the principle is that you ought, prima facie, to keep your promises. More precisely, it means that, if you have promised to do something, that gives you a moral reason to do what you have promised to do. If you have no other reasons, then you should do what you have promised to do. If you have other reasons, then you must weigh your various reasons in order to decide what you ought to do all things considered.

For example, you have promised to attend a meeting, but your aunt has just died so you also have an obligation to attend her funeral. You therefore have conflicting obligations. Given that you have promised to go to the meeting, you ought (prima facie) to go to the meeting. Given that your aunt has died and your parents will be expecting you at the funeral, you ought (prima facie) to go to the funeral. These "ought" statements do not contradict each other, since they are prima-facie "ought" statements. Neither statement says what you ought to do all things considered. This can be determined only by weighing your reasons and deciding which is stronger.

Ross's theory of the prima-facie "ought" makes a great deal of sense from the point of view of the good-reasons analysis. In his view, moral principles indicate what you have moral reasons to do. What you should do, all things considered, is not determined by some further moral principle but is determined in whatever way conflicting reasons are weighed against each other, be they moral reasons or reasons of other sorts.

Putting this in another way, we might take Ross's theory to be a remark about the logical form of "ought" statements. Strictly speaking, we can say, an "ought" statement has the form, "Relative to C, P ought to do D." For example, "Relative to the fact that you have promised to do something, you ought to do it." An all-things-considered "ought" judgment would then have the form, "All things considered, P ought to do D"—in other words, "Relative to all things considered, P ought to do D." This amounts to the claim that the prima-facie "ought" is basic and that the all-things-considered "ought" is to be defined in terms of the prima-facie "ought." We might then define the basic, prima-facie "ought" like this: "Relative to C, P ought to do D" means the same as "C gives P a reason to do D."

Exactly similar remarks can be made about the "ought" of expectation. There is a prima-facie "ought" of expectation and an all-things-considered "ought" of expectation. We say, "Going by the timetable, the train ought to be here in five minutes; but, given that the engineer is new at the job, the train ought to be somewhat later than that." We can define the basic form of the "ought" of expectation as follows: "Relative to C, it ought to be that S" means the same as "C is a reason to believe that S." Analogously, we might define the basic form of the evaluative "ought as follows: "Relative to C, it ought to be that S" means the same as "C is a reason to wish or hope that S."

Finally, consider the "ought" of simple rationality. Kant holds that moral requirements derive from reason alone; according to him it is irrational not to act morally. If that were true, there would be no reason to distinguish the moral "ought" from the "ought" of simple rationality. And, even if we suppose that Kant is wrong about the powers of reason, we might still suppose that the moral "ought" is a special use of the "ought" of rationality—not that it is irrational to fail to act in accordance with the moral law but rather that moral "ought" judgments are judgments using the "ought" of rationality made about agents who are believed to intend to adhere to the relevant moral principles.

The basic logical form of an "ought" statement, using the

"ought" of rationality, is "Relative to C, P ought to do D." The suggestion is that this is the moral "ought" if the conditions C include P's intending to adhere to the relevant principles. In that case, in saying "Relative to C^1, P ought morally to do D" we are saying "Relative to the fact that C^1 and that P intends to adhere to the relevant principles, P ought to do D." According to this suggestion, the difference between the judgment that the bank robber ought to give up his trade and the judgment that the bank robber ought to use the rear door is that in the former judgment but not in the latter we take the relevant conditions C to include the bank robber's acceptance of certain principles. What we mean is that, given his acceptance of those principles, he has reasons to go home rather than to enter the bank and rob it.

This is to reduce the moral "ought" to the "ought" of rationality. Analogous reductions of the other "ought's" can also be given. The "ought" of expectation in "Relative to C, it ought to be that S," becomes "Relative to C, one ought to believe that S." The evaluative "ought" in "Relative to C, it ought to be that S," becomes "Relative to C, one ought to hope or wish that S."

It still makes sense to say that the word "ought" has four different meanings, since these reductions are not the same from one case to the next. A sentence of the form "Relative to C, P ought to do D" might mean any of four different things, which can be expressed using the "ought" of rationality as follows: "Relative to C, P ought to do D," "Relative to C and that P accepts the moral conventions we accept, P ought to do D," "Relative to C, one ought to believe that P does D," "Relative to C, one ought to hope or wish that P does D." These are not equivalent. Nor is it quite correct to say that the moral "ought" is just a special case of the "ought" of rationality. The difference is that when we use the "ought" of rationality to say that P ought to do D, we are not necessarily endorsing P's doing D, but, when we use the moral "ought" to say that P ought to do D, we are (normally) endorsing P's doing D. When I say that a bank robber ought to use the rear door, I do not endorse his doing so; I am not indicating that I am in favor of his doing so. But, when I say that the bank robber ought to give up his trade, I do endorse his doing so; I am indicating that I am in favor of his giving up his trade. The moral "ought" is therefore the "ought" of rationality plus something else. When I use the moral "ought," I presuppose that the agent and my audience accept certain practical principles that I also accept, and I make my judgment relative to those principles.

Consider also the ways in which we react on learning that an agent does not have the goals we assumed he had. I judge that a bank robber ought to use the rear door because I suppose that his goal is to rob the bank and get away unobserved. If I learn that he does not intend to rob this bank but is merely making a deposit, then I withdraw my judgment that he ought to use the rear door and I say that I was mistaken. On the other hand, suppose that I use the moral "ought" to say that the bank robber ought to give up his trade. In saying this, I am presupposing that certain principles that the bank robber accepts give him reasons to stop being a bank robber. If I learn that the bank robber is, however, totally amoral and that, given his goals and plans, he has absolutely no reason not to continue being a bank robber, then although I will withdraw my judgment I will not do so by saying that I was *mistaken*. This difference indicates that the two sorts of judgment are not of the same kind. The moral sense of "ought" is distinct from the sense of the "ought" of rationality, even though the two senses are closely related.

4. Some complications

It is an oversimplification, by the way, to speak of the *moral* "ought," since the same sense of the word is used when it is said that someone has reasons to do something relative to rules of law, club rules, conventions of etiquette, rules of a game, and so forth, which the speaker takes the agent to accept. If, for example, it turns out that the agent does not accept those rules or conventions, the speaker will not withdraw his original statement by saying that he was mistaken. The fact that "ought" has the same sense in all of these cases is additional support for the social convention theory of morality. Given that theory, it seems appropriate to say that those who accept rules of law, club rules, or conventions of etiquette accept them in the way they accept moral conventions.

Another complication is that the moral "ought" can be used relative to a morality that the speaker does not share and, in that case, in judging that P ought to do D, the speaker does not necessarily endorse P's doing D. Consider such judgments as these: "You, as a Christian, ought to turn the other cheek; I, however, propose to strike back." A spy who has been found out by a friend might say,"I hope that you will not turn me in, although I realize that, as a loyal citizen, you ought to do so." In such a case, if it turns out that the agent is not a Christian, or is not a loyal citizen, the speaker can withdraw his original judgment by saying that he was mistaken. The difference between the moral "ought" and the "ought" of rationality does not emerge in such examples; it emerges only in the more usual case in which the speaker shares the relevant principles and endorses P's doing D.

A note on further reading

R. M. Hare's theory is explained in *The Language of Morals* (Oxford: Oxford University Press, 1952) and in *Practical Inferences* (Oxford: Oxford University Press, 1971).

Kurt Baier defends a good-reasons analysis in *The Moral Point of View* (Ithaca, N.Y.: Cornell University Press, 1958), Chapter 3—"The Best Thing To Do."

W. D. Ross discusses the notion of a prima-facie duty in *The Right and the Good* (Oxford: The Clarendon Press, 1930), Chapter 2.

Donald Davidson treats Ross's idea as an insight about logical form in "How Is Weakness of the Will Possible?" in Joel Feinberg (ed.), *Moral Concepts* (Oxford: Oxford University Press, 1969).

Philippa Foot notes resemblances between the moral "ought" and the "ought" of etiquette, etc., in "Morality as a System of Hypothetical Imperatives," *Philosophical Review*, Vol. 81 (1972).

11 A naturalistic theory of reasons

1. Reasons and reasoning

If a good-reasons analysis of the type described in the previous chapter is successful, moral "ought" judgments can be explained in terms of judgments using the "ought" of rationality, and these judgments can in turn be explained as remarks about reasons. But this would not by itself yield a naturalistic reduction of moral judgments to judgments about facts of nature. For one thing, there are other moral judgments besides "ought" judgments and related judgments using "may" and "must." There is the judgment that Hitler was an evil man, for example, and we have not said anything about how a judgment like that might be analyzed (nor will we say anything about that in what follows). Furthermore, although a good-reasons analysis reduces moral "ought" judgments to judgments about reasons. these judgments about reasons are themselves normative judgments and therefore not clearly judgments about facts of nature. Nevertheless, if a good-reasons analysis is successful, we may well feel that some progress has been made.

Reasons probably have something to do with someone's possible reasoning. It might be suggested that for someone to have (good) reasons to do something is for there to be (good) reasoning "available" to him that would lead him to decide to do that thing. Let us pursue that suggestion. Then in order to say what it is for someone to have certain reasons to do something, we must say what it is for there to be certain reasoning "available" to him. This means that we must say something about what reasoning is and also something about what it is for reasoning to be "available" in the relevant way. Let us begin by considering an inadequate account of these matters and then turn to a more adequte one.

2. Reasoning as proof or argument

The inadequate account takes an instance of reasoning to resemble a proof or an argument, with premises, steps of reasoning, and a conclusion. Reasoning is more or less conclusive, so we are to assume that there are arguments of various strengths. The strongest argument is a *deductive* argument, in which each step is guaranteed to be true given the truth of the premises or prior steps from which it is derived by means of a principle of deductive logic. One such principle says that *not* S and S *or* T logically imply T. In other words, the truth of *not* S and of S *or* T guarantees the truth of T. If it is true that Albert is not coming to the party and also true that either Albert or Mabel is coming, it is guaranteed to be true that Mabel is coming to the party.

Not all reasoning is conclusive in this way; not all reasoning is deductive. So, if an instance of reasoning is to resemble a proof or an argument, there must be nondeductive or *inductive* arguments, which contain steps that are supported but not guaranteed by the premises or earlier steps from which they are derived. Such a step would have to be derived by means of a principle of *inductive logic*. There is, however, no general agreement about the principles of inductive logic, so I cannot give a clear example of such a principle. I will return later to the problem that this raises.

We have so far considered only reasoning that leads you to accept a belief. There is also practical reasoning, which leads you to decide to do something. So there must also (in this view) be practical arguments of varying strengths, with conclusions that are statements of intention or, perhaps, imperatives.

Summing up, then, according to this conception of reasoning, we see that there are not only deductive arguments but also weaker inductive arguments, as well as practical arguments of various strengths, with conclusions that are, say, decisions to do something. Deductive logic is, in this view, the theory of deductive reasoning. There is also an inductive logic, which serves as a theory of inductive reasoning, as well as one or more practical logics to provide an account of practical reasoning. In Hare's theory, for example, the "logic of imperatives" is a theory of practical reasoning. In this kind of theory, then, reasoning is available if you accept the premises of that reasoning—for in that case you are justified in also accepting the conclusion of that reasoning if you do so by reasoning from those premises by running through the relevant steps of reasoning or proof.

This account of reasoning is inadequate because it misconstrues the relation between reasoning and logic. There are deductive arguments and proofs, but there is not deductive reasoning—not in the logician's sense of "deductive" anyway. Deductive principles of logical implication are not to be confused with principles of reasoning or of inference. We have discussed the logical principle that *not* S and S *or* T logically imply T. This does not mean that if you believe *not* S and also believe S *or* T, you are entitled to conclude by believing T. Sometimes you should instead give up one of the premises of your argument. Similarly, it is a principle of standard deductive logic that inconsistent premises logically imply anything and everything; and this does not mean tht if you discover that your beliefs are inconsistent you are entitled to respond by believing anything and everything.

Reasoning can lead you not only to accept new beliefs, goals, desires, plans, and so forth, but to reject some of your antecedent beliefs, goals, plans, and desires. Therefore, reasoning is not best thought of as argument or proof, with premises, steps of reasoning, and a conclusion. Rather, you start out with a set of beliefs, plans, goals, desires, and intentions, which you modify as the result of reasoning, adding to and subtracting from this set as appropriate. To speak of the reasons you have is to speak of reasoning you could do that would lead you to modify your total set of beliefs, plans, goals, desires, and intentions.

Logic is concerned with argument and proof and not directly with reasoning. Logic is sometimes relevant to reasoning, because argument and proof are sometimes relevant. But argument and proof are not the same as reasoning. An argument, or a proof, resembles an explanation more than an inference. Argument can be relevant to reasoning because it can have an explanatory function and because explanations are often relevant to reasoning. In reasoning you often seek to improve the explanatory coherence of your overall view.

There are deductive arguments and proofs, but there is no such thing as deductive reasoning. There is inductive reasoning, but no need for any special inductive logic, since there are no inductive arguments in the way that there are deductive arguments. The logic relevant to inductive reasoning is simply deductive logic, which is, strictly speaking, the only kind of logic there is. Deductive logic is relevant to inductive reasoning, because inductive reasoning is often inference to the best explanation and explanation often takes a deductive form.

Following Aristotle, we might call inductive reasoning "theoretical reasoning." Theoretical reasoning is reasoning concerned with belief; whereas what Aristotle called "practical reasoning" is concerned with desire or intention. To say that someone has certain reasons to do something is to say that he has practical reasoning available to him that would lead him to decide to do it. The same old deductive logic is, however, as relevant to practical reasoning as it is to inductive or theoretical reasoning. There is no special practical logic, no logic of imperatives, no practical syllogism. Logic is relevant to practical reasoning to the extent that explanatory coherence is relevant. In practical reasoning you try to make your plans more coherent internally and more coherent with your goals and desires. This coherence is at least partly explanatory, since, among other things, your plans specify how you plan to do things, and that is to purport to explain how you are going to do those things. Such explanations can take a deductive form.

3. A better account of reasoning

The theory of reasoning is therefore not to be identified with logic. The theory of reasoning, if such a theory is possible at all, is a normative subject. Logic is not in the same respect a normative subject, although, as I have suggested, it is relevant in certain ways to the normative theory of reasoning.

An instance of reasoning might be identified simply as the transition from a set of antecedent beliefs, plans, goals, desires, and intentions to the modified set that results. In general, no particular reasoning is absolutely required by rationality at any given time. Ordinarily, any of a number of different changes in your antecedent view might be acceptable. You are not forced to reason in one way only. You might reason this way or that way or the other way.

This possibility of choice accounts for the practical use of such words as "may," "ought," and "must." So, for example, you have a sufficient reason to do D if there is an acceptable change in your views of this sort that includes your coming to decide to do D (or continuing to intend to do D). In that case, at the very least, you *may* or *might* do D. Sometimes reasoning that would involve your deciding to do D (or continuing to intend to do D) is clearly preferable to other reasoning available to you, although that other reasoning is still possible without being actually irrational. In that case, you *ought* to do D, although you do not *have* to do D. On the other hand, if it would be irrational for you not to reason in such a way that you decide to do D (or continue to intend to do D), then you *must* do D—you *have* to do it.

What is required for certain reasoning to be acceptable reasoning? In order to answer this question, we might hope to state certain explicit general principles of reasoning in the same way that we are able to state explicit general principles of deductive logic, and so develop a rigorous normative thoery of reasons. It is unlikely, however, that such a theory is really possible. There is no more evidence that there are explicit general principles of reasoning than that there are explicit general principles of aesthetic appreciation.

4. The ideal reasoner

We might also hope for a naturalistic reduction of statements about reasons and reasoning in the way that statements about colors are reduced to statements about ideal observers or statements about the average citizen are reduced to statements about citizens in general. Perhaps we could say something like this: Reasoning is acceptable if it is reasoning that an ideally functioning reasoner might reason, an ideally functioning reasoner being anyone whose reasoning is not distorted or misfunctioning in one or another way. This would be a theory that is in a certain sense intermediate between the ideal observer theory of morality and a theory that analyzes "ought" and "good" in terms of roles, functions, and interests (as discussed in Chapter 2). One objection to the ideal observer theory of moral judgments would not apply, however, to this ideal reasoner theory of reasoning, namely the objection that the ideal observer theory does not bring out the way in which morality involves an appeal to principle. There can be no analogous objection to the ideal reasoner theory of reasoning, because reasoning does not appeal to principles of reasoning in the way morality appeals to moral principles. (Of course, reasoning often appeals to principles—principles of logic, of science, of morality, and so forth. The point is that these are not principles of reasoning.) On the other hand, to make the ideal reasoner theory work, it might seem that we would have to further analyze what it is to reason without distortion or misfunction; and it is not clear how we might give such an analysis at the present time. So it may seem to be unclear whether such a naturalistic reduction is possible.

But we do not need to be able to further analyze what it is to reason without distortion or misfunction. Recall that ethics is problematic because alleged moral facts do not seem to play a role in explaining why anyone makes the particular observations he makes. Moral observaitons are properly explained, it seems, by an appeal to the observer's moral principles and moral sensibility rather than facts about what is really right or wrong. Furthermore, someone who does something because it is right does something that seems to be explained by an appeal to that person's belief that it is right rather than to the actual rightness of what he does. On the other hand, judgments about reasons are not problematic in the way moral judgments are. We often appeal to purported facts about reasons in order to explain why people do what they do or believe what they believe. We explain why someone does something or believes something by giving what we take his reasons to be.

Such explanations, in terms of a person's reasons, presuppose something like the crude theory of reasons and reasoning described above. According to this theory, there is a certain sort of psychological process that might be called a process of reasoning—coming to believe something for certain reasons, or coming to intend to do something for certain reasons. The theory does not contain explicit general principles of reasoning; nor does there seem much chance of our soon discovering such principles. Therefore, in order to see whether certain reasons or reasoning might explain a particular person's beliefs or actions we must try to imagine ourselves in his position, with his antecedent beliefs, desires, moral principles, and so forth, to see whether we can imagine what sorts of conclusions we might draw by reasoning from that position. This appeal to the sympathetic imagination is necessary, because we cannot appeal to explicit principles of the theory of reasoning to tell us what reasoning is possible and what is not. We can, however, rely on our imagination in this way only if we can assume that our reasoning works in the same way the other person's reasoning works. We must therefore assume some sort of ideal reasoner theory. Our theory of reasons and reasoning must involve the claim that the process of reasoning is universal and always the same from person to person, except when it is distorted or malfunctioning in on or another way. This is, of course, an empirical hypothesis; one that might be challenged. But it is difficult to see how we could suppose that we could ever explain why people believe as they do or behave as they do, in terms of the reasons they have, unless we could assume that some sort of ideal reasoner theory is correct. In any event, the theory of reasons is an empirical theory—that is the important point.

5. Moral facts

To be sure, there remain questions about the ultimate scientific status of alleged facts about reasons, just as there are questions about the ultimate status of psychological facts. We might well wonder, for example, how alleged facts about reasons are related to the facts of physics, chemistry, and biology. But there is no special problem here—only a general issue about the relation between psychology and the physical sciences.

The theory of reasons and reasoning is, therefore, not particularly problematic—at least no more so than any other part of psychology. And that means that ethics may not be so problematic either—once moral relativism is taken into account. For suppose that the convention theory of morality and a good-reasons analysis are both correct. Then, although there are no absolute facts of right or wrong, apart from one or another set of conventions, there is evidence that there are relative facts about what is right or wrong with respect to one or another set of conventions. For these facts would be facts about whether or not those who accept certain conventional practices have reasons to do one or another thing; and there is empirical evidence that there are such facts about reasons, because we often must appeal to facts about reasons in order to explain why people do as they do and why they believe as they do. Therefore, there is empirical evidence that there are (relational) moral facts.

The idea that moral facts are relational facts about reasons is more plausible than Kant's view that moral facts are nonrelational facts about reasons, although we have not refuted Kant. In Kant's view, moral facts are facts about reasons people have to do things—reasons they have whether or not they accept certain conventions. Kant could, of course, agree that accepting a convention affects the reasons you have; he certainly would also say that there are moral reasons to adhere to many of the conventions of your community—you ought to cooperate with others, everything else being equal. Kant might even accept the explanation that the social convention theory gives concerning the intuitive moral difference between harming and not helping. Kant could agree that this intuitive difference results from the fact that our conventions are a compromise that has been tacitly worked out between people of different powers and resources; he would only add that the real moral significance of the difference derives from the moral reasons that we have for adhering to the conventions of our society.

Kant could also accept an ideal reasoner theory of reasons; his disagreement with the social convention theory is a disagreement over the powers of reason. Kant held that any rational being has reasons to refrain from injuring others, to be honest and truthful, to provide help to those who need it, and so forth. According to Kant, even a Martian or a Hitler or an amoral member of Murder, Inc. has such reasons (if he is a rational being). In the social convention theory, on the other hand, this is not true.

The two views therefore differ over the source of moral reasons. Kant sees their source in the nature of reason itself—that is, in the nature of the reasoning process. In the social convention theory, reasoning is not taken to itself possess such power: the source of moral reasons is the aims and goals of the person involved. We feel, I think—at least, I feel—that the social convention theory must be right about the powers of reason. Kant asks too much of reason. The burden of proof is on Kant to show how reason could have the powers he attributes to it; and so far neither Kant nor anyone else has been able to show this. This does not mean that Kant is wrong; but, on the other hand, it seems unlikely that he could be right. In any event, we must now look more closely at possible sources of moral reasons. Let us begin, then, by considering egoism, in the next chapter.

A note on further reading

For more discussion, see Gilbert Harman, *Thought* (Princeton, N.J.: Princeton University Press, 1973), especially Chapter 10, and "Practical Reasoning," *Review of Metaphysics*, Vol. 29(1975–76).

R. M. Hare treats the "logic of imperatives" as a theory of inference in his *Practical Inferences* (Oxford: Oxford University Press, 1971).

V

Oneself and others

12 Egoism

1. Self-Interest

We have seen that certain moral judgments are plausibly interpreted as judgments about moral reasons. It is now time to say something about the possible sources of these reasons. Let us begin by considering in some detail a theory called egoism, which holds that practical reasons of any sort, including moral reasons, derive ultimately from considerations of self-interest. In this theory, you have reasons to tell the truth and keep your promises only to the extent that you can reasonably assume that honesty is the best policy. You must be able to assume that God or society or your own conscience will reward you for honesty and punish you for dishonesty. You might, for example, have some reason to think that other people will want to cooperate with you in ways that are in your interest only if you deal honestly with them.

It may seem at first that egoism is a relatively clear and precise theory. The concept of self interest, however, is vague in a way that introduces a kind of vagueness or even ambiguity into what is to count as egoism. It will not do, for example, to say simply that something is in your interest to the extent that it satisfies, rather than frustrates, your desires. The fact that you desire something does not, in itself, show that getting it would be in your interest. You might ignorantly desire something that is not in your interest, because you are mistaken about what effect it would have. We must therefore say, rather, that something is in your interest to the extent that it satisfies, rather than frustrates, your *intrinsic* desires, where you desire something intrinsically if you desire it for its own sake and not just because of any consequences you think, possibly mistakenly, that it may have.

But even this is not enough to count as the sort of egoism I want to discuss. You can certainly have an intrinsic desire for pleasure; and some people would say that only pleasure can be desired intrinsically. The difficulty is that there are other people who assume you can also have intrinsic desires for various other things. They would say, for example, that, if you are in love with someone, you will have an intrinsic desire for that person's happiness; you will want that person to be happy quite apart from any effect his happiness will have on you. This would mean, in terms of the suggested definition of self-interest, that anything that promotes that other person's happiness is in your "interest" even if it has no effect on you whatsoever—even if you never know about it. That is too loose an interpretation of self-interest for my purposes. Egoism defined in terms of such self-interest would be too broad a view. That sort of "egoism" would be compatible with the most generous altruism, if you had an intrinsic desire to make other people happy. Given that desire, you would thus have a "self-interested" reason to promote the general welfare. I want, however, to consider a more restricted idea of self-interest and a correspondingly narrower conception of egoism. An egoist in my sense will deny that *intrinsic* desires for the happiness of others are possible. A nonegoist, in my sense, can agree that your reasons for action must derive ultimately from your intrinsic desires, because he may think that you can have intrinsic desires that are not self-interested. They are *your* desires, of course, but that does not necessarily make them self-interested. Hume, for example, believes that, because of the powers of sympathy, people are sometimes capable of unselfish concern for others and that this concern can provide you with (weak) reasons to act so as to benefit others apart from any expected gain for yourself. Hume is, therefore, not an egoist in my sense, even though he supposes that all of your reasons for action derive from your intrinsic desires. But it is not obvious how the more restrictive form of egoism I want to consider is to be defined.

We might try to explain self-interest in terms of happiness saying that something is in your interest to the extent that it promotes your happiness and diminishes your unhappiness. But what is happiness? If happiness is getting what you want, this account of self-interest reduces to our earlier account. If it is possible to have an intrinsic concern for other people, the general welfare might constitute part of your happiness apart from any effect on you, given an unnaturally wide conception of happiness. We need a narrower conception.

2. Egoistic hedonism

How, then, is happiness to be defined? It is often said that happiness consists in pleasure and the absence of pain. So, the most popular version of egoism (and the only version we shall consider) is egoistic hedonism, the theory that all desire is ultimately desire for your own pleasure. In this view, pleasure—your own pleasure—is the only thing you desire intrinsically. You cannot have an intrinsic desire for someone else's happiness; at best you can have an intrinsic desire for the pleasure that you would get from the other person's being happy, either because, if the other person is happy, he will be nice to you, which will give you pleasure, or because you will get pleasure from the thought that the other person is happy.

Such a theory gains a certain amount of plausibility from considerations of motivation theory and learning. A newborn baby is a total hedonist; it seeks only to obtain pleasure and avoid pain. As it grows older, it continues to seek pleasure, but it learns to delay gratification. Instead of some pleasure now, the child learns to aim at more pleasure later. Parents educate and socialize the child by rewarding certain of its actions and penalizing others. This works because the child desires the pleasurable rewards and wants to avoid the painful penalties. As a result of this parental training, the child comes to desire new things, not intrinsically, of course, but because it has learned that those are connected with pleasure and the absence of pain. The child comes to want to behave in certain ways, not because it comes to have intrinsic desires to behave in those ways, but because it has been rewarded with pleasurable experiences for such behavior and has been punished by painful experiences for other behavior. As an added dividend, furthermore, there is the pleasure of anticipation: The thought of certain rewards is itself pleasurable; so pleasurable thoughts become directly associated with the actions the child has been rewarded for performing. The child may even repeat those actions for that pleasure alone, long after its parents have stopped rewarding it.

There are, it is true, examples that apparently conflict with egoistic hedonism as a theory of adult motivation. But these are not conclusive. An extreme example is that of someone who commits suicide in order to "get back" at others by making them feel bad. This presents a problem, because it is hard to see how the person who commits suicide could expect to get any pleasure from the act itself. Psychologists explain the difficulty by supposing that anyone who commits suicide for this sort of reason must be unconsciously assuming that he is somehow going to be around afterwards to enjoy the other person's suffering and that they invoke unconscious assumptions of this sort to explain away other apparent contradictory examples. They say, for example, that people make wills partly because they get some pleasure before the event of thinking of how they have arranged things, partly because of the pleasure they can get by showing the wills to those who are mentioned (or not mentioned), and partly because they irrationally imagine that they will somehow be aware of what happens after they are dead and will, after all, be influenced by what happens then.

You hope that you will be remembered after you die, according to egoistic hedonism, because you think of death as a kind of life. First of all, you like to be thought of while you are alive. It gives you pleasure to know that others are thinking of you and there are the indirect benefits of fame: people like to talk to you; they invite you to their parties. Irrationally, you unconsciously suppose that posthumous remembrance and fame will be like that. You imagine, irrationally, that you will still be there to benefit from your posthumous remembrance and fame.

As observed in Chapter 5, we can similarly invoke the Freudian theory of the superego. When you were young, your parents rewarded you for acting in certain ways and punished you for acting in other ways. You learned after some time to imagine what your parents would say about various courses of action.

You imagine them disapproving of some courses and approving of others. You then do something that you think they would approve of and you pretend that they are there rewarding you. This pretense gives you pleasure even though it is only a pretense. Eventually, you routinely act so as to receive the imagined praise and rewards of a fictional parent, your superego, although you are not consciously aware that this is your reason.

3. A standard objection

There is, however, a standard objection to any form of egoistic hedonism that is defended by an appeal to unconscious beliefs and motives. The objection is that, if egoism is defended in this way, it becomes untestable and unscientific; if egoistic hedonism is thus defended, we cannot even imagine a case of human behavior it could not account for, which means that it can make no real empirical claim about human behavior.

Consider, for example, a case of wartime heroism.

A group of soldiers are trapped behind enemy lines. One of them volunteers to run into the open to draw the enemy fire so that the others can escape. The volunteer believes he is quite certain to be killed. Furthermore, he is an atheist, who does not believe in life after death. He is also a hard-headed realist; he does not suppose, for example, that after he is killed his soul will float about the battlefield where it can witness the escape of his friends and hear their praise of his noble action.

Would such a case, if it occurred, refute egoistic hedonism? Obviously not! For one thing, the soldier may be thinking that he could not live with himself later if he did not do what he promised to do. He may therefore sacrifice himself thinking that in this way he will avoid future pain. But then, let us build into our description of the case that this is not true.

The soldier realizes full well that he would not suffer a great deal if, instead of running into the open so as to draw away the enemy fire, he were to hold back and hide behind the nearby trees so that the enemy would locate his friends and, in the battle that follows, he would be able to escape although his friends would die as a result. He would later feel some regret about this, but he will still be able to get much happiness out of life. Memory is merciful. He knows that he is not the sort of person to dwell on such things. He knows that he would not suffer very much if he cheated and let others get killed rather than himself. Nevertheless, knowing all this, he runs into the open, draws the enemy fire, and is killed, while his friends escape.

Would that refute egoistic hedonism?

It would not. An advocate of that theory can always postulate, as a last resort, that despite the soldier's professed atheism and conscious belief that there is no afterlife, he is *unconsciously* assuming that he will be around later to see and hear the escape of his friends and hear their praise of him. Unconsciously, the soldier thinks that he will get a great deal of pleasure out of his action, since unconsciously he thinks that he will be around after the event. There is also the pleasure he irrationally imagines that he will get as a reward from his superego; here there is a double fiction involved. His superego is an imaginary parent and, anyway, neither he nor his superego will be around after the event. Furthermore, he may unconsciously exaggerate how bad he would feel if he were not to do what he promised to do.

The fact that egoistic hedonism can accommodate such cases is not obviously a point in its favor. On the contrary, it seems to show that the theory can make no empirical claim at all about human behavior. Things would be different if the theory predicted, for example, that only nonatheists would act in the way described. Then the theory would predict that, in the situation described, an atheist would not actually run into the open in order to attract enemy fire but would instead hide behind the trees and let his friends get killed by the enemy. A theory that made such a prediction would be an interesting empirical theory that could be tested by examining cases of heroism. (The theory would probably be refuted.) But an egoistic hedonism that is defended by an appeal to unconscious irrational beliefs cannot be tested this way. It therefore may seem to make no interesting empirical claims about human behavior, because it may seem to be compatible with any imaginable human behavior whatsoever. This in any event is a standard objection against egoistic hedonism, when it is defended in the way I have suggested.

4. Reply to the objection

The objection is not well taken, however. It is based on the assumption that the empirical content of a claim rests entirely on its testable consequences. The difficulty with this assumption is that it will count almost any scientific statement as empirically meaningless. Few such statements are testable in isolation from other assumptions. A single statement about the mass of electrons, for example, has no verifiable consequences taken by itself. The statement makes no empirical claim about the observable behavior of macro-objects. We are able to obtain evidence for or against hypotheses about electrons only because we make certain assumptions about other particles and about our tools for measuring. If all these assumptions, taken together, allow us to make an empirical prediction about what we are going to observe, and that prediction is not fulfilled, we may decide that our assumption about the mass of the electron is wrong, or we may instead give up one or another of our other assumptions. If we wanted to, we could continue consistently to accept any hypothesis at all about the mass of electrons, as long as we were willing to make other assumptions to account for observations, not that this would always be a rational thing to do.

The point is that we do not evaluate individual hypotheses in the light of empirical evidence; we evaluate whole theories. Even though egoistic hedonism, taken by itself, has no testable consequences, it may nevertheless be a useful part of a larger theory, which itself is very fruitful. And, when egoistic hedonism is thus treated as a scientific hypothesis—in other words, when it is treated as an assumption in theory—then in order to decide whether or not it is true—that is, whether or not we want to accept it) we must not simply ask whether there is some direct way to test that particular hypothesis; we must instead compare the theory, of which egoistic hedonism is taken to be a part, with other theories that do not involve egoistic hedonism.

Looking at egoistic hedonism as part of a more extensive theory—such as Freudian theory—we can understand its merits. For one thing, as we have seen, it yields a simple account of the way motivation develops. The appeal that the theory must make to unconscious beliefs and desires is, furthermore, really a strength rather than a weakness. People *are* motivated in unconscious ways that they do not fully understand and may not recognize. They are often enmeshed in irrational patterns of behavior that constantly recur, over and over again, patterns that sometimes make sense only on the assumption that the agent is acting toward other persons as if they were his parents or siblings. But that is just to say that we can make sense of a great deal of otherwise irrational seeming behavior only if we attribute certain unconscious beliefs and desires to people.

Again, in considering how egoistic hedonism would explain suicides and acts of heroism, we saw how it might appeal to the unconscious belief that the agent was going to be around after his death. There is evidence that this is right. For example, when the agent decides to do something in order to hurt someone else, the agent often does think over in great imagined detail just how the other person is going to feel, and in imagining this, the agent imagines himself somehow knowing about it even in cases in which he is fully aware that he will never know.

The theory of the superego also has a great deal in its favor. People do tend to talk to themselves—blaming themselves, encouraging themselves, praising themselves, and so forth— in ways that might be appropriate for parents or parental substitutes. As we noted in Chapter 5, it is a familiar fact that athletes tend to internalize their coaches so that they address themselves, sometimes even out loud, as a harsh coach might. Furthermore, the authority of the coach is itself often best explained by supposing that the coach has in some way replaced a parent. One acts toward the coach the way one might act toward an idealized parent.

5. What do people want

We are not, however, concerned with whether Freudian theory, or some other similar theory, is roughly correct but are concerned, more specifically, with egoistic hedonism. I have described as Freudian a theory that takes the basic source of motivation to be a desire for pleasure and the absence of pain. In fact, that is true only of Freud's earlier theory, based on the pleasure principle. Later Freud himself came to think that egoistic hedonism did not offer a plausible explanation of certain kinds of destructive behavior and he therefore postulated the existence of a second drive, *Thanatos*, a kind of death wish. The relevance of this is that we can keep much of Freudian theory or of some related theory while varying assumptions about the basic drives or sources of motivation. What we want to compare (among other things) are theories that are basically like Freud's theory in that they appeal to unconscious motivation, parent figures, superegos, and so forth, but that make different assumptions about basic drives and intrinsic desires. Two possibilities were therefore both put forward by Freud himself, egoistic hedonism and his later dualistic theory.

Other psychologists have suggested other possible basic drives, such as curiosity. Thus, it is possible that a baby is born with an innate desire to know things, quite apart from any pleasure that it may receive from that knowledge. A Freudian might say, on the other hand, that curiosity is learned: the child is rewarded for learning things and generalizes this, perhaps by adding imaginary rewards. It is not obvious how we would decide between these theories. A rat that has never been rewarded for running through a maze will still explore one it has been placed in. Does this show that the rat has an innate drive to know things? Is its curiosity innate? The Freudian—or the Skinnerian—might say that what is innate is not curiosity but a connection between obtaining certain kinds of knowledge and obtaining pleasure; the rat and baby are curious because they obtain pleasure from learning new things. How can we decide between these theories? How are people constructed? Evolution has worked in such a way that people adapt to the world around them. To effect this, evolution has ensured that we will be curious. But has it done this by building in a special curiosity drive or has it done this by making the acquisition of knowledge pleasurable? And is there a real difference between these apparent alternatives? These are difficult questions and it is not clear that philosophy can answer them.

The newborn baby has desires for food at certain times and desires for water. Evolution has designed the baby so that when its body is in a certain state it will be hungry, and when its body is in a different state it will be thirsty. How does this work? Should we suppose that hunger and thirst are basic drives that are triggered in the baby by the relevant body states? Or should we suppose that the baby is motivated to get the pleasure of filling its stomach in certain ways and is motivated to end the discomfort it feels when it is hungry or thirsty? Either of these mechanisms seems a possible one; it is not obvious how we might discover which is the actual one.

It is not easy to say whether hunger is a desire to eat or a desire for the pleasure of eating. But there are desires that do not appear in any obvious way desires for the pleasure that accompanies their satisfaction. Indeed these pleasures appear to depend on a previous desire. A man takes pleasure, for example, in the happiness of his children, because he wants them to be happy. It is not normally true that he wants them to be happy because that makes him happy. Although it does make him happy, his happiness depends on his prior desire for his children's happiness. The object of that desire is their happiness, not his own. His own happiness is derived from his desire's satisfaction; it is not what his desire is a desire for. Or so it would seem. Egoistic hedonism must treat this appearance as illusory.

Love and friendship also seem to be things people want for themselves, over and above the pleasures involved. Consider someone who imagines that he has several close friends who like him very much and a wonderful wife and children who love him, although actually the children are not his, his wife despises him, and his so-called friends only tolerate him because they are paid to do so. He never discovers this. He lives to be 75 years old and dies without ever having the slightest suspicion. He dies a happy man. Or does he? His life definitely seems to have lacked something very important, something that he wanted very much and thought he had. This would seem to indicate that what a person wants can transcend his pleasures and subjective experiences. Most people would prefer a life in which their friends really did admire them and their wives or husbands really did love them. They would prefer such a life to one that was subjectively the same in which, however, they were not really loved and admired but were secretly despised. This suggests that a person's true interests should not be identified with the pursuit of pleasure, because people are interested in more than that. People desire more *for themselves,* it seems, than pleasure; often what pleasure they have is the result of their believing that their desires for other things are satisfied. According to egoistic hedonism, these desires are irrational; but why should we agree?

People do seem genuinely capable of motivation that is not self-interested. Psychological hedonism—indeed any form of egoism—must treat these desires as irrational and foolish—like those of a miser who has forgotten the point of having money and who has come to desire money for its own sake; rich but miserable he counts his wealth, constantly worried lest someone try to steal it from him. But the fact that it is sometimes irrational to act out of non-self-interested motives does not mean that it always is. There are other cases in which we think highly of a person who is motivated by what appear to be considerations other than self-interest. A fireman saves a family in a burning building only to perish in the flames. A prisoner refuses to talk under torture, even though it would clearly be in his interest to do so. A soldier volunteers for a "suicide mission" in order to save his friends. We admire such people and even hope that we will be able to act in that way if the occasion should ever demand it. According to egoism, when we think like this, we are deluded.

There are many examples of this sort of thing that do not involve any sort of heroism. A stranger asks you how to get to Nassau Hall. You tell him, although it is not particularly in your interest to do so. It seems right to tell him and wrong not to, or to tell him something false. Normally we would suppose that you had some reason to tell him where Nassau Hall is; this reason would not appear to derive from your own self-interest. The egoist must deny that there is any such reason.

If egoistic hedonism is true, you only have a reason to do whatever will best satisfy your desires for pleasure and the absence of pain. But if egoistic hedonism is not true and there are other things you desire for their own sake, then it would seem that you can have a reason to do whatever will satisfy these other desires. These other desires might well involve the happiness of other people. Someone asks you how to get to Nassau Hall: you have an intrinsic desire to help him—so you have a reason to tell him how to get to Nassau Hall. The fireman realizes that there are children trapped in the burning building: he immediately acquires an intrinsic desire that they should be saved—so he has a reason to enter the building and lower them from the second floor window, even though this involves risking his own life.

The egoist wants to know how you can have a reason to act in someone else's interest if that reason does not derive from your own self-interest. The answer is that you can have such a reason if you care about that person for his own sake. You can have such a reason if you have an intrinsic desire for that person's happiness.

The egoist takes it to be obvious that there are reasons to do what is in your self-interest and wonders how there can be reasons of any other sort, altruistic reasons for example. But, as philosophers have observed, if there is a puzzle as to how there can be altruism, there is equally a puzzle about self-interest. Why should you care about other people? Well, why should you care about what happens to you? A person may just not care, for one or another reason, either about what happens to someone else or about what happens to himself. In that case, reasons of altruism or of self-interest will have no appeal. This is often true of reasons of long range self-interest for most people. You have a reason derived from your long range self-interest not to smoke; yet you smoke—you do not care that much about what it is going to be like for you 50—or 20—years from now. Reasons derive from your desires, what you care about. If you care about your future self, you have self-interested reasons to act in various ways. If you do not care about your future self, you may not have any such self-interested reasons. If you care about others, you have other regarding reasons to act in various ways; if you do not care about other people, you may not have such reasons to act in those ways.

How can you have reasons that do not derive from self-interest? You may first, as Hume believed, have reasons that derive from an innate sympathy and concern for others that evolution has built into you. Furthermore, considerations of self-interest may lead you to develop non-self-interested concerns. For one thing, there is a matter of efficiency. It is useful for you to have a good reputation as someone who can be trusted. If people do not think that you are fairly certain to pay back what you have borrowed, they will not lend you money. If people do not think that you are honest, they will not trust you. If people do not think that you are kind and generous, they will not feel kindly and generously disposed toward you. But one way to have a good reputation is to become the sort of person you want to have the reputation of being. If you make it a rule always to be honest in your dealings with others, always to pay back your debts, to be kind and generous, to help others when they need help, and so forth, this is likely to be noticed by others and you are likely to acquire the reputation you want. This may well be the best way to go about acquiring that sort of reputation, since it is difficult to be calculating all the time and since any slip could completely undo months and even years of careful planning. You therefore have a powerful reason to act morally even in cases where it seems quite unlikely that anyone could ever know that you were not so acting. But that is to say that you have a self-interested reason to develop a concern to act morally even

acting morally is not in your self-interest on a particular occasion.

There are also self-interested reasons of a different sort for one
to develop intrinsic concerns for others. The life of someone
who is concerned with other people is likely to be a much happier life than the life of someone who is mainly self-interested.
If you care about others, then your life will be more interesting, more varied, more exciting. Their happiness will lead
to your happiness. You will not be subjected to the destructive agonies of competition. In competing with others, if you and
they are self-interested, one person wins, the others lose. Most
are therefore made unhappy. If instead you and the others are
concerned not only with yourselves but with each other as well,
then there is no real competition. If any of you gains, you all
gain, because you will all be happy about that person's success.

6. How non-self-interested desires can arise

What bothers the egoist about this, even if he believes it, is that
he does not see how anyone could develop genuinely non-self-
interested concerns. The egoist argues, for example, that, if you
develop a concern for others because it is in your interest to do
so, your concern must ultimately be a concern for your own
interests and cannot be a genuinely non-self-interested concern
for someone else.

But this is to assume wrongly that, if you form a desire for F
because you want E, your desire for F is ultimately a desire for
E; it is to assume that you can form such a desire for F only
because you believe that F will lead to E. There are, however,
other cases the egoist overlooks. You can, at least for a short
time, simply take an interest in something or adopt a desire for
something, not because of what you expect to get from that
thing itself but from what you expect to get from being
interested in it. You can want F because you want E, where you
expect to get E not from getting F but from wanting to get F.
This is easy to overlook because it is such a common phenome-
non. It manifests itself all the time in games and other forms of
play. You temporarily adopt a desire to win, because it is more
fun playing if you are trying to win than if you are not. You take
an interest in the topic of conversation, not because information
on that subject will advance your antecedent interests, but be-

cause you get more pleasure out of a conversation if you are interested in what is being discussed.

Out of purely self-interested motives you could develop a genuine long lasting concern for others. Taking an interest in someone for his own sake is not difficult; we do it all the time if only to make our contacts with others more bearable. The difficulty is maintaining such an interest over time. You have to go through the motions over and over again until it becomes habitual. Then, by the same psychological principle of generalization that leads the miser to become habitually interested in money for its own sake rather than for what it can buy, you may find yourself habitually taking an interest in other people for their own sake and not just for your own benefit. Paradoxically, in thus casting away your egoism and becoming concerned with others, you act in your own interest and help make yourself happy.

A growing child acquires many non-self-interested concerns with little conscious calculation. This is only natural. It is only natural for children to play, to come to love their parents, and to develop other interests. The egoist is right in seeing that the development of these concerns is in the child's interest; he may even be right in thinking that the child develops these concerns because it is in its interest to do so; but that is no argument for egoism. It does not follow that these concerns are ultimately concerns for the child's own interests. The child—perhaps for self-interested reasons, perhaps for other reasons—develops genuinely non-self-interested concerns. Having developed those concerns, the child and the adult he becomes can have genuinely non-self-interested reasons for doing things—reasons that may even make it rational, given a person's present concerns, to do things that are not in that person's interests. Egoism is not all of human motivation. Not all reasons are reasons of self-interest.

7. Can moral reasons be self-interested?

This by itself does not show that moral reasons are non-self-interested. People can have reasons of self-interest to adhere to certain conventions. If those conventions are moral conventions, which give participants moral reasons to do things, it might be argued that certain participants might have moral reasons to do things that are, for them, ultimately reasons of self-interest.

Other participants might adhere to the same conventions out of love and concern for others; for them, moral reasons would not be reasons of self-interst.

On the other hand, it might not be possible genuinely to adhere to certain conventions without acquiring intrinsic concerns for others. A convention of respect for participants in a convention might be such a case. A morality that involved such respect would necessarily yield moral reasons that were not reasons of self-interest—even for people who participated because they had self-interested reasons to do so.

It is, furthermore, a plausible hypothesis about our use of the word "moral" that conventions are correctly called moral conventions only if they are conventions of respect for participants. This would explain why conventions of language and rules of the road are not properly considered part of morality. Given this hypothesis and the social convention theory of morality, it would follow almost by definition that moral reasons are based on concern for others and not on self-interest.

This conclusion is intuitively plausible by itself, apart from considerations of theory. We ordinarily suppose that someone who acts solely out of self-interest does not act from a moral reason. Kant's example is a storekeeper who gives the right change because it is in his interest to be known to have that policy. The storekeeper does the right thing, but we would not normally think that he was doing so for reasons of morality. To act for reasons of morality is to act, not out of self-interest, but out of an intrinsic concern and respect for people as "ends in themselves."

A note on further reading

There is a classic critique of egoistic hedonism in Bishop Joseph Butler's *Fifteen Sermons Preached at the Rolls Chapel*, especially Butler's Preface and Sermons 1 and 11.

There is also a useful discussion of egoistic hedonism in Richard B. Brandt, *Ethical Theory* (Englewood Cliffs, N.J.: Prentice-Hall, 1959), pp. 307–314.

C. G. Hempel discusses "Empiricist Criteria of Cognitive Significance" in *Aspects of Scientific Explanation* (New York: Free Press, 1965).

Signund Freud's later theory of motivation is developed in *Beyond the Pleasure Principle* (New York: Norton, 1961).

Michael Scriven describes how self-interest can lead to the adoption of moral attitudes in *Primary Philosophy* (New York: McGraw-Hill, 1966), Chapter 7.

13 Utilitarianism

1. Utilitarian reasons

Moral reasons are not reasons of self-interest. They derive from an intrinsic concern or respect for others as well as yourself. I have suggested that this concern or respect is required by certain social conventions. Kant held, on the other hand, that it is required by pure practical reason. He thought that a rational being must feel such concern or respect for other rational beings by virtue of being rational. Kant was, however, never able to prove that this is so and we may be pardoned for doubting it. Yet another theory might state that concern or respect for other people derives from an innate human sympathy, which is itself to be explained in terms of evolution.

What sorts of things might your concern or respect for others give you moral reasons to do? The simplest and most famous theory is *utilitarianism*, according to which you have a moral reason to do whatever will best promote the general welfare. Utilitarianism is sometimes described as the theory that you ought always to act so as to maximize social utility, where "social utility" is simply another name for the general welfare. This way of putting things will do for the time being, although, as we will see, it is possibly misleading. Apart from verbal quibbling, however, the basic idea behind utilitarianism should be clear.

It is often said that utilitarianism conflicts with our ordinary views. This conflict is, however, less than it may seem at first. Where there is conflict, moreover, utilitarianism may appear on reflection to be more reasonable than our usual convictions.

Consider promises, for example. Our ordinary view is that to promise is to put yourself under an obligation to do what you have promised to do. The obligation is not absolute; there are cases in which you are justified in making a lying promise; and there are cases in which, having made a sincere promise, circumstances arise in which you ought to do something else than keep your promise. Nevertheless, our ordinary view is that promises make a moral difference. The fact that you have promised to do something is at least a reason to do that thing, even if this reason is occasionally overridden by other reasons. It may seem, however, that utilitarianism is not compatible with this. Utilitarianism is, it seems, a "forward looking" rather than a "backward looking" view. What is important, according to utilitarianism, is not what has happened in the past, but what might happen in the future as a consequence of the various things you might do. It would seem to be irrelevant what you once promised to do; you should now do whatever will now best promote social utility, even though you may have promised to do something quite different.

Promises can, however, make a difference, even for a utilitarian, since promises themselves have consequences. There is, as it happens, a practice in our society of keeping promises that one has made. When you promise to do something, therefore, you tend to create, in the person to whom you have made your promise, an expectation that you will do the thing in question, and he will adjust his plans accordingly. In that case, if you do not do what you have promised to do, you will disappoint him and frustrate his plans. If you had not made your promise, he would not be counting on you. The consequences of your not doing something will therefore often be different depending on whether or not you promised to do it; so it would be wrong to say that, according to utilitarianism, promises make no moral difference. They do make a moral difference, because they make a difference to the consequences of later actions, and consequences make a moral difference, according to utilitarianism.

Continuing to adhere to your practice of keeping promises is also useful in another way: it encourages people to trust you in the future. If people stopped trusting you to keep your promises, it would become harder for you to coordinate your actions with theirs, and the things that you could do in order to promote utility would be greatly reduced. In considering whether you ought to keep a particular promise, of course, you must consider not only the direct effects of various courses of action open to you but also any indirect effects, for example, on your continuing ability to coordinate your actions with others in the future. In most cases, this consideration is sufficiently important to give you a powerful utilitarian reason to keep your promise.

2. Explaining non-utilitarian intuitions

The two factors I have mentioned, having to do with the expectations of the person to whom you have made your promise and, in addition, your ability to continue to use promises to coordinate your actions with others in the future, are not involved, however, in cases of what are sometimes called "desert island promises." Suppose, for example, that you and another person are shipwrecked on a desert island and the other person is dying. Before he dies, he gives you a sum of money and makes you promise that, if you are rescued, you will give the money to a certain Austin Jones, his unacknowledged illegitimate son. You promse; he dies content; and shortly afterward you are rescued. On returning home, you discover that Jones is a well-off but extremely selfish man and it becomes immediately clear to you that much more good would come of the money of it were to go to some useful charity rather than to Jones. What should you do?

You are certainly not going to disappoint anyone's expectations. The only other person who knew about the promise is now dead. What you do will, therefore, have no effect on his welfare. Jones, on the other hand, knows nothing about your promise and therefore has no expectation to be disappointed if you do not give him the money. Furthermore, since no one knows you made that promise, your failing to keep it will have no effect on anyone's future trust in you to keep promises. You might even lie and say that you had promised that you would see to it that the money would go to CARE. In giving the money to CARE, in that case, you would reinforce the trust that others have in your reliability. It·would therefore seem that, from a utilitarian point of view, the fact that you made a promise should be totally irrelevant. You should do what is best and that is the same as what it would have been best to do if you had not made your promise. You should give the money to Jones, as you promised to do, only if that would also have been the right thing to do with the money even if you had not promised. Since giving the money to Jones would not have been the right thing to do, you should break your promise and give the money to CARE.

Here, however, there is a clear conflict between utilitarianism and ordinary moral opinion. Ordinarily we would suppose that a promise, even a desert island promise to a dying man that no one else knows about, has some moral weight. To be sure, the promise does not have an absolute weight, but it has *some* weight, we ordinarily suppose. But, according to utilitarianism, in this case, the promise has no weight. That is counter-intuitive.

The utilitarian reply to this complaint is to agree that the utilitarian conclusion is counter-intuitive but to maintain that it is nevertheless correct. The utilitarian conclusion is counter-intui-tive in the sense that any ordinary person in this situation will feel some motivation to do what he has promised to do, namely to turn the money over to Jones, and may even feel guilty if instead he gives the money to CARE. This is because he has been trained to keep his promises and to feel guilty if he does not. There is, furthermore, a good utilitarian reason to train people in this way rather than to try to train them to act like rational utilitarians. For, in many cases, it is not clear what the right thing to do is from a utilitarian point of view. It is therefore useful to have rules of thumb for deciding what to do rather than having each person in each case begin from the beginning. If, furthermore, people were trained to decide what to do in each case as it came along, they would be likely to make many disastrous mistakes. Important utilitarian considerations are often complex, indirect, and easily overlooked—for example the indirect effects of promise-keeping already noted. It is therefore useful to train people so that they will follow general rules except when it is absolutely clear that utility would be maximized by acting in some other way. Once people are trained thus to follow general rules, they may have intuitions that occasionally conflict with utilitarianism and they may feel guilty for acting against those intuitions even if, as good utilitarians, they know that they are doing what is really the right thing to do. So, even though utilitarianism conflicts with ordinary views about desert island promises, it can give an explanation of our ordinary feelings about such cases, an explanation of why we might rationally have those feelings even though the right thing to do is different from what we would ordinarily take it to be.

Other non-utilitarian intuitions we have might be explained similarly. There is, for example, the intuitive moral distinction that we recognize between harming someone and not helping someone; we think that a doctor should not cut up one of his patients in order to save five other patients, although from a utilitarian point of view that is just what the doctor ought to do. The utilitarian will have to say that our natural intuitive judgment about this example is mistaken; he can, however, explain why we have such intuitions and why it is rational, from a utilitarian point of view, to train people so that they will have such non-utilitarian reactions. For there is a utilitarian point to distinguishing harming from not helping in many cases. The point is that what will help someone is often a matter of that person's particular goals, which vary from one person to another. To go around trying to help people is often to do more harm than good; it is often to interfere rather than to help. It is usually clear enough, on the other hand, that a given course of action will harm someone. Therefore, as a useful rule of thumb, there is often a stronger utilitarian reason to try to avoid harming others than to try to help them. Helping others is a good thing, from a utilitarian point of view, but what constitutes help is not always as clear as what constitutes harm. Someone who tries to help others runs the risk of being an interfering busybody, or worse. Not knowing the goals and aims of another person, you may wrongly project on that person your own goals and aims. Considerations of self-interest on your part can lead to further distortion. Therefore, from a utilitarian point of view, you and others should be trained so that you are strongly motivated to avoid actions that might harm others and are motivated to try to help others only when it is quite clear that you are helping and not just interfering. Given this training, however, you will make an immediate intuitive distinction between harming and not helping someone. You will, for example, judge that the doctor should not harm one patient in order to help five other patients.

This judgment is wrong, from a utilitarian point of view. There is, however, a utilitarian explanation of why you should be trained to make it.

3. Does utilitarianism require too much?

We have been considering how utilitarianism might meet the objection that it sometimes recommends courses of action that are intuitively wrong. There is also an opposite objection: utilitarianism asks too much of us. For utilitarianism says that you always ought to do that act that will maximize utility and it is extremely rare for anyone ever to do that. Consider your own present situation. You are reading a philosophical book about ethics. There are many courses of action open to you that would have much greater social utility. If, for example, you were immediately to stop reading and do whatever you could to send food to places like Africa or India, where it is scarce, you could probably save hundreds, even thousands of lives, and could make life somewhat more tolerable for thousands of others. That is something you could do that has a greater utility than anything you are now doing; it probably has a greater utility than anything you are ever going to do in your whole life. According to utilitarianism, therefore, you are not now doing what you ought morally to be doing and this will continue to be true throughout your life. You will always be doing the wrong thing; you will never be doing what you ought to be doing. That conclusion is very different from any ordinary view of the matter. Utilitarianism implies that it is morally wrong of you to be reading this book. That is not the sort of thing people ordinarily think of as morally wrong.

Someone who acted in the way recommended by utilitarianism would not be a good example of a person doing what one ought morally to do, as we ordinarily conceive of such a person. A utilitarian agent would be very different from most of us. He would be a saint or a super Ralph Nader. At every moment such a person would do what seemed to him to have the best change of maximizing utility. He would occasionally rest; but only so as to be able to return to the battle with renewed vigor. This is an inspiring picture, but it is not our picture of someone who does what he ought to do; it is our picture of someone who does much more.

The utilitarian theorist might reply that the fact that we are weak and lazy and not willing to do what it is clearly desirable to do is no argument against utilitarianism. It is no argument against the supposition that we ought morally to do what it is clearly desirable to do. It would clearly be better to be working actively to reduce and eliminate starvation than to be reading philosophy. You ought morally to be working to reduce starvation and it is morally wrong of you to continue reading this book, even though you are too lazy to do what you morally ought to do.

This utilitarian reply is not fully satisfactory, however. We can agree that what utilitarianism recommends is or would be wonderful. It would be wonderful if any of us were to act in the way that utilitarianism says that we ought to act. But does that mean that we are morally *required* to act that way? The point is that utilitarianism appears to obliterate certain distinctions. We ordinarily suppose that there are differences between saying that it would be wonderful for P to do D, that it would be nice of P to do D, that P ought to do D, that P is obligated to do D, that P has a duty to do D, and that P must do D. We ordinarily suppose, for example, that there are circumstances in which it would be nice if someone were to do something, although it is not the case that he has a duty to do it or even ought to do it. It would be very nice of you to buy me lunch; you are, however, not obligated to do so and it is not even true that you ought to do so. If you and I regularly buy each other lunch, on the other hand, and I am a little short today, perhaps you ought to buy me lunch, even though you are still under no obligation or duty to do so. Here are distinctions of the sort that we make all the time in our ordinary moral thinking; it would seem that there is no place for them in utilitarian thinking if the only issue is what will maximize utility. It may seem that, for a utilitarian, whatever maximizes utility must be simultaneously what it would be wonderful to do, what it would be nice to do, what one ought to do, what one must do, what one is obligated to do, what one has a duty to do. No wonder utilitarianism has seemed to many, many philosophers to be an extremely crude theory.

I have already mentioned another distinction we ordinarily make that utilitarians believe has significance only as a practical rule of thumb, the moral distinction between harming and not helping someone. Here again, the utilitarian way of talking appears to lead to curious conclusions. Failing to save someone's life would seem not to be any different, in utilitarian morality, from actually killing someone. Since any of us could, if we tried, save many people's lives, in not doing what we can to save those lives we are apparently no better than murderers, from the utilitarian point of view. The utilitarian must apparently suppose that we are no different morally from the commander of a concentration camp who gasses hundreds of prisoners.

It may seem therefore that utilitarian morality turns out to be a curiously abstract discipline with little of the complexity of our ordinary moral thinking: we are all mass murderers; we always act wrongly; we never do what we morally ought to do.

4. A utilitarian account of ordinary moral distinctions

But in fact utilitarian account of morality can allow us to make many of the moral distinctions we would ordinarily like to make by considering when, from a utilitarian point of view, it would be appropriate to praise or blame someone. We ordinarily distinguish, for example, between things a person ought to do and other things that it is not the case he ought to do but that it would be nice of him to do or wonderful of him to do. The utilitarian might explain this as a distinction within the class of things a person ought to do between things that deserve praise if done and other things that do not deserve praise if done. Similarly, for some things but not other things you ought to do, you ought to be blamed if you do not do them. Where we would ordinarily say that P ought to do D, the utilitarian might say simply that P will deserve blame for not doing D. Where we would say that it would be nice of P to do D, even though P does not have to, the utilitarian might say simply that P will deserve mild praise if P does do D. Where we see a moral distinction between someone who reads this book, thereby failing to save hundreds of lives by working for famine relief agencies, and the person who heads a concentration camp and puts hundreds of prisoners to death, the utilitarian can see a difference in the sort of condemnation these different acts deserve. In either case, the utilitarian might say that the agent is doing something that he ought not to be doing, but the utilitarian may well see a utilitarian reason for wanting to condemn the actions of the person who runs the concentration camp more than the actions of the person who is reading this book rather than working for famine relief.

Utilitarianism conceives morality as a matter of benevolence.

The moral motive is altruistic and other-regarding. In an ideal state of affairs, everyone would be perfectly benevolent; everyone would always count others' interests as important as his own. People are, however, not yet like that; and it is possible that they never will be. The purpose of praise and blame, from a utilitarian point of view, is to encourage people to act more benevolently than they do and less self-interestedly than they do. People like to be praised and do not like to be blamed. They are therefore motivated to act so that they will be praised and not blamed. But this is only one motivation. There are others. People are motivated to act so that they will be praised and not blamed if they can do so fairly easily and without much trouble. If we praised people only when they acted so as to maximize expected utility and blamed people whenever they did not, our praise and blame would be counter-productive. Since it would require too much effort for people to receive praise and avoid blame, they would lose interest in trying to do so. As people are now, they have reached a compromise between the claims of benevolence and self-interest. People are self-interested and, to some extent, benevolent. The purpose of praise and blame is to encourage people to become more benevolent and less self-interested. We do this by praising actions that are more benevolent than we usually expect from people and by blaming actions that are less benevolent and more self-interested than those we usually expect from people. In this way, we hope to coax people into moving toward the moral end of things and away from the self-interested end. But this all depends on our not placing the standards of praise and blame too high. Otherwise, people would just ignore our praise and blame, since it would be too hard for them to be praised and not blamed.

5. Utilitarianism as an ideal

I have been writing as if utilitarianism is best expressed as the theory that one ought morally to do whatever will maximize expected utility. But now an alternative terminology suggests itself. We might say that what someone ought to do, according to utilitarianism, is anything that there are utilitarian reasons to blame him for not doing; it would be nice (or good) of someone to do anything that there are utilitarian reasons to praise; and so forth. This terminology allows the utilitarian to distinguish things that it would be nice for someone to do from things that he ought to do, using these words in something like their ordinary sense.

What utilitarianism says we ought to do may therefore be closer to our usual opinions than it seemed at first. For, when utilitarianism is reformulated in the way I have just suggested, it is not obviously committed to saying that the doctor ought to cut up the one patient to save five other patients, because blaming the doctor for not doing this will almost certainly be counter-productive. Nor is it committed to saying that you are wrong to be reading this book instead of working for famine relief. You are acting much as most people do, so there is probably little to be gained from blaming you for what you are doing. It will probably be better to praise those who go into famine relief than to blame those who do not.

But, even if utilitarianism does not obviously conflict with our considered moral views in what it says we ought to do, there is still an important respect in which it does not give an adequate account of our morality. Utilitarianism might be construed as the theory that moral reasons derive entirely out of a concern for the general welfare. It is clear from the way in which utilitarianism must be defended, however, that we can have moral reasons that derive from other concerns. In explaining our intuitive feelings about desert island promises, for example, utilitarianism notes that each of us has been brought up to care, intrinsically, about keeping his promises. This intrinsic concern can give someone a reason to keep a promise quite apart from considerations of the general welfare. Such a reason is, surely, a moral reason. It is, therefore, a moral reason that does not arise out of a concern for the general welfare.

Our attachment to promise-keeping is not irrational, from a utilitarian point of view, because it promotes the general welfare. The utilitarian cannot say, therefore, that we ought to abandon this concern, which gives us moral reasons that are not derived from an interest in the general welfare. Furthermore, the fact that there is this utilitarian justification of our concern does not mean that the concern itself is really a concern for the general welfare, anymore than the fact that there is a justification of this concern in terms of self-interest means that the concern is a self-interested concern.

We accept many other moral conventions in the way that we

accept the conventions associated with promises. We have an immediate intrinsic concern to act according to these conventions. The original spur to our developing such a concern was probably self-interest. It was in our interest to develop that concern and to be known to have done so. Since the general welfare is simply the sum of the interests of all, there is also a utilitarian reason for us to continue to have that concern. But again, this does not mean that our moral concern is self-interested or even, typically, a concern for the general welfare.

Moral reasons derive not only from our concern for others but also our respect for them. What does that mean? Kant suggested that it means respect for a law to which we and they have agreed. We might say that it is respect for the moral conventions of our society. Those conventions define our conception of respect. We do not eat human flesh; to do so would in our society indicate a lack of respect for the person eaten and for people generally. For us, to harm someone intentionally is to show a lack of respect for him that failing to help him does not show, other things being equal. Often, indeed, attempts to help people in our society will be interpreted as indicating a lack of respect for the people involved. Many people are, for example, "too proud" to go on welfare. Things would be different in a more egalitarian society that did not morally distinguish harming from failing to help someone as we do. In such a society, failing to help someone would be as much a sign of disrespect as harming someone.

Respect for others involves some concern for them. So there is pressure toward utilitarianism. Self-interest leads us to adopt conventions of respect and concern. Our concern for others will then give us reasons to improve our conventions so as to better promote the general welfare. In this way, we make moral progress, our self-interest giving way to benevolence in the way utilitarianism recommends. Still, we remain self-interested. That keeps a rein on morality and keeps us from going all the way in the direction of unilateral benevolence and altruism.

A note on further reading

For classic statements of utilitarianism, see Jeremy Bentham's *Introduction to the Principles of Morals and Legislation* and John Stuart Mill's *Utilitarianism.* For a more recent defense, see J. J. C. Smart, "Extreme and Restricted

Utilitarianism," in *Philosophical Quarterly*, Vol. 6 (1956) and his contribution to J. J. C. Smart and Bernard Williams, *Utilitarianism: For and Against* (Cambridge: Cambridge University Press, 1973).

Name index